Angels, Demons and Spiritual Warfare

Trevor Newport

New Wine Press

New Wine Press
PO Box 17
Chichester
West Sussex PO20 6YB
England

Unless otherwise stated, all Bible quotations are from The King
James Version – Crown copyright.

ISBN: 1 874367 59 0

Typeset by CRB Associates, Reepham, Norfolk
Printed in England by Clays Ltd, St Ives plc.

Contents

PART ONE

Angels

Chapter 1

Introduction

I want to begin by saying that, as Christians, we do not look for angels. Nor should we bow down to them. Neither should we engage in any form of demon-hunting or try to take the place of God. Rather, we should take our example from Jesus Christ. As Paul says:

> *'Let this **mind** be in you, which was also in Christ Jesus: who, being in the form of God, thought it not robbery to be equal with God: but **made himself of no reputation, and took upon him the form of a servant**, and was made in the likeness of men: and being found in fashion as a man, **he humbled himself**, and became **obedient unto death**, even the death of the cross. Wherefore **God also hath highly exalted him, and given him a name which is above every name**: that **at the name of Jesus every knee should bow**, of things **in heaven** and things **in earth**, and things **under the earth**: and that **every tongue should confess that Jesus Christ is Lord**, to the **glory of God the Father**.'*
>
> (Philippians 2:5–11)

Notice carefully in verse 10 that every knee will bow to

Jesus in heaven which means every angel ever created has to bow to Him.

Then it says, *'things in earth'*. This means every man, woman and child will one day have to bow the knee to **Jesus Christ** either in this life (as Saviour) or in the next (as their Judge).

The third phrase in verse 10 then says, *'things under the earth'* will have to bow their knee to **Jesus Christ**. Every principality of darkness, every unclean spirit, every devil, every demon, every spirit of infirmity, every ruler of darkness, Beelzebub and Satan will one day bow their evil knee in the midst of the Lake of Fire and declare that **Jesus is Lord!**

However, the Word of God does tell us to *'seek those things which are above, where Christ sitteth on the right hand of God'* (Colossians 3:1). The Bible also tells us that we should be *'looking unto **Jesus**, the author and finisher of our faith'* (Hebrews 12:2a). We are to worship the Father and His Son Jesus Christ through the help of the Holy Spirit (John 4:23; Philippians 3:3; Psalm 45:11).

We are to honour Jesus Christ at all times and give Him our highest praise because He is:

The Prince of Peace   (Isaiah 9:6)
The Mighty God   (Isaiah 9:6)
Wonderful Counsellor   (Isaiah 9:6)
Holy One   (Mark 1:24)
Lamb of God   (John 1:29)
Prince of Life   (Acts 3:15)
Lord God Almighty   (Revelation 15:3)
Lion of the Tribe of Judah   (Revelation 5:5)
Root of David   (Revelation 22:16)
Word of Life   (1 John 1:1)
Advocate   (1 John 1:1)
The Way, the Truth, the Life   (John 14:6)

Dayspring from on High   (Luke 1:78)
Lord of All   (Acts 10:36)
The Great I AM   (John 8:58 etc.)
Son of Man   (Luke 6:5)
Son of God   (John 1:34)
Shepherd and Bishop of Souls   (1 Peter 2:25)
Messiah   (John 1:41)
Saviour   (2 Peter 2:20)
Chief Cornerstone   (Ephesians 2:20)
Righteous Judge   (2 Timothy 4:8)
Light of the World   (John 8:12)
Head of the Church   (Ephesians 1:22)
Morning Star   (Revelation 22:16)
Sun of Righteousness   (Malachi 4:2)
Lord Jesus Christ   (Acts 15:11)
Chief Shepherd   (1 Peter 5:4)
Resurrection and Life   (John 11:25)
Horn of Salvation   (Luke 1:69)
Governor   (Matthew 2:6)
The Alpha and Omega,
   the Beginning and the Ending   (Revelation 1:8)
The King of Kings and
   Lord of Lords   (Revelation 19:16)

He is Jesus Christ of Nazareth, the Son of the Living God! You can never exalt or magnify Him enough. Jesus Christ must remain the central focus of our entire existence.

'O come let us adore Him, Christ the Lord!' Hence, the object of this book is **not** to take anyone's attention away from the Lord, but rather to equip the body of Christ and to heighten her awareness of supernatural activity both in people's lives and in the heavenlies.

My prayer for you as you read this book is that it will stir your heart to have a much deeper walk with the Lord to the point where He will start to reveal more and more of His miraculous power and entrust you with signs, wonders and miracles to glorify Jesus!

Remember:

> *'Yea, all of you be subject one to another, and be clothed with humility: for **God resisteth the proud, and giveth grace to the humble. Humble yourselves therefore under the mighty hand of God, that he may exalt you in due time**: casting all your care upon him; for he careth for you. Be sober, be vigilant* (to keep awake, watchful)*; because your adversary the devil, as a roaring lion, walketh about, seeking whom he may devour: whom resist steadfast in the faith, knowing that the same afflictions are accomplished in your brethren that are in the world. But the God of all grace, who hath called us unto his eternal glory by Christ Jesus, after that **ye have suffered*** (i.e. trials, testings, persecutions etc.) *a while, make you **perfect, stablish, strengthen, settle you.** To him be glory and dominion for ever and ever. Amen.'* (1 Peter 5:5–11)

Chapter 2

The Doctrine of Angels

*'Are they not all ministering spirits, sent forth to minister **for them who shall be heirs of salvation?'***
(Hebrews 1:14)

This verse from Hebrews gives us one of the main functions of angels: angels are ministering spirits.

When Jesus was tempted by the devil in the wilderness, we read in Matthew's account:

*'Then the devil leaveth him and, behold, **angels came and ministered unto him.'***　　　(Matthew 4:11)

I believe that when we as Christians go through times of testing, angels come and minister to us after we have overcome the lusts of the flesh, the cares of this life etc. Having said this we must also understand that there are different kinds of angels performing different duties.

Seraphim

'In the year that King Uzziah died I saw also the Lord sitting upon a throne, high and lifted up, and his train

> *filled the temple. Above it stood the seraphims: each*
> *one had six wings; with twain he covered his face, and*
> *with twain he covered his feet, and with twain he did*
> *fly. And one cried unto another, and said, Holy, holy,*
> *holy, is the LORD of hosts: the whole earth is full of his*
> *glory.'*   (Isaiah 6:1–10)

Looking closely at the function of the seraphim, it is clear that they stand above the throne of the Lord which is already *'high and lifted up'*. Each individual seraphim has six wings: three sets of two. The first two wings cover its face, the next two its feet and the third pair are used for flying (verse 2).

In verse 7 we see that the seraphim are able to communicate with each other verbally. The next verse is also very interesting because even the door posts move at the seraphims' cry and the house is filled with smoke.

In verse we see that the seraphim are not fixed to one particular location but in fact are mobile. Isaiah watches (presumably with awe and amazement) as one of these angelic beings flies to him from heaven and takes *'a live coal in his hand, which he had taken with the tongs from off the altar.'* The Word speaks for itself:

> *'And he* (the seraphim) *laid it upon my mouth, and*
> *said, Lo, this hath touched thy lips, and thine iniquity*
> *is taken away, and thy sin purged.'*   (Isaiah 6:7)

Thus the seraphim performs a delegated duty of cleansing (purging) Isaiah's sin and then the Lord speaks and says, *'Whom shall I send, and who will go for us?'* (The plural 'us' meaning the Father, Son and Holy Spirit.) Isaiah responds to the Lord and says, *'Here am I; send me'* (verse 8).

This wonderful passage of Scripture gives us an insight as to the close working relationship that the Godhead has with seraphim. In the book of Revelation, we are given another glimpse of the seraphim:

> *'And before the throne there was a sea of glass like unto crystal: and in the midst of the throne, and round about the throne, were four beasts full of eyes before and behind. And the first beast* (seraphim) *was like a lion, and the second beast like a calf, and the third had a face as a man, and the fourth beast was like a flying eagle. And the four beasts had each of them six wings about him; and they were full of eyes within: and they rest not day and night, saying, Holy, holy, holy, Lord God Almighty which was, and is, and is to come.'*
>
> (Revelation 4:6–8)

We then see a chain reaction as the 24 elders *'fall down before him that sat on the throne . . . '* etc. (verse 10).

Cherubim

In Genesis chapter 3 we read the account of the fall of Adam and Eve in the garden. After God had disciplined Adam, Eve and the serpent (Satan), He removed Adam from the garden:

> *'Therefore the Lord God sent him forth from the garden of Eden, to till the ground from whence he was taken. So he drove out the man; and he placed at the east of the garden of Eden* **Cherubims**, *and a flaming sword which turned every way, to keep the way of the tree of life.'* (Genesis 3:23–24)

This is the first mention of angels in the Bible. It seems that God placed on guard cherubim and a flaming sword to prevent anyone partaking of the tree of life. No doubt this is the mercy of God to prevent anyone taking of the tree of life and living for ever in their sinful condition (see Genesis 3:22). God wants us to live with Him forever in righteousness not sin. Thus the cherubim were placed on guard duty.

In 2 Samuel 22:7–11 we read that David was in great distress and cried unto the Lord for help. Verse 11 says,

> *'And he* (the Lord) *rode upon a **cherub**, and did fly: and he was seen upon the wings of the wind.'*

Thus cherubim are used as heavenly transport for the Lord Himself.

One of the most graphic portions of Scripture on cherubim is found in Ezekiel chapter 10:

> *'Then I looked, and, behold, in the firmament that was above the head of the cherubim there appeared over them as it were a sapphire stone, as the appearance of the likeness of a throne. and he spake unto the man clothed with linen, and said, Go in between the wheels, even under the cherub, and fill thine hand with coals of fire from between the cherubims, and scatter them over the city. And he went in my sight.'* (Ezekiel 10:1–2)

Read the whole chapter.

Verse 21 gives a description of these heavenly beings:

> *'Every one had four faces apiece, and every one four wings: and the likeness of the hands of a man was under their wings.'*

I wonder what they must look like in reality! Maybe you could make a sketch of what they look like if you are good at drawing. Please send me a drawing if you do!

Archangel – the Chief Messenger

Archangel is actually mentioned twice in Scripture: in 1 Thessalonians 4:16 and Jude 9. In Jude we are given a specific name:

> *'Yet **Michael the archangel**, when contending with the devil he disputed about the body of Moses, durst not bring against him a railing accusation, but said, The Lord rebuke thee.'*

The word 'arch' means chief or principal. Therefore Michael is the principal angel.

Gabriel

We are not given many names of angels in the Bible but Gabriel is mentioned in both Daniel in the Old Testament and also Luke in the New Testament: Daniel 8:16; 9:21; Luke 1:19, 26. Luke records:

> *'And the angel answering said unto him, I am Gabriel, that stand in the presence of God; and am sent to speak unto thee, and to shew thee these glad tidings.'*
> (Luke 1:19)

If you compare this verse to those regarding the seraphim it looks likely that Gabriel is a seraphim.

Angels in General

The greater part of the ministry of angels is in heaven (see Revelation chapters 4 and 5). They are God's servants fulfilling His will by carrying out the commands of the Lord. Angels do not need redemption from sin as humans do. Angels differ in size and strength (compare Revelation 10:1 to Acts 12:15 for instance). Their appearance to men is for special occasions historically but they are seen during most if not all revivals.

Old Testament Appearances

Hagar (Genesis 21:17); Abraham (Genesis 18); Lot in Sodom (Genesis 19); Jacob in dreams and reality (Genesis 28:12; 32:1–2). Also when Jacob wrestles with a *'man'* (Genesis 32:24–30) this is at least an angel if not the Lord Jesus Christ Himself.

As the children of Israel were led through the wilderness they were accompanied by an angel of God (for example Exodus 14:19). It was angels who arranged the Old Testament law (Acts 7:53). Angels can be seen by animals when not seen by men (Numbers 22:22–35); the donkey of Balaam. Angels can preach to men (Judges 2:1–4) and often stood by faithful servants of the Lord to encourage and strengthen (Judges 6:20–23). It was an angel that announced the birth of Samuel (Judges 13:15–23). Angelic visitations were certainly not restricted to the Old Testament. For example, the opening of prison doors was by an angel in Acts 12:10.

Thus angels are able to perform miracles to accomplish God's purposes on the earth. However, they can never work independently. Rather they are under the commands of the Lord, often through the prayers of believers (Psalm 103:20–21).

Not only do angels perform 'pleasant' duties, but they are also seen when God has to bring judgement. Angels brought strict discipline to Israel in David's time and the plagues in Egypt. The Passover was a very sombre time for Egypt when the angel brought death to all the first born.

In Acts 12:23, we see the death of Herod carried out by an angel of the Lord because *'he gave not God the glory.'* Pride brought the ultimate fall! I thank God that He protects faithful believers at all times by surrounding us with angels and delivering us from unseen dangers (Psalm 34:7; 35:5–6).

An interesting verse is found in the book of Ecclesiastes:

> *'Suffer not thy mouth to cause thy flesh to sin; neither say thou before the angel, that it was an error: wherefore should God be angry at thy voice, and destroy the work of thine hands?'* (Ecclesiates 5:6)

Even in the lions' den we see Daniel testifying about angels being sent by God to *'shut the lions' mouths'* (Daniel 6:22). Praise God for angels! We are never alone. We have God the Father, God the Son, God the Holy Spirit in us and with us, along with different kinds of angels to guide, protect, warn, comfort, strengthen or chastise us! I am glad to be a Christian!

New Testament Appearances

As we turn our attention to the New Testament (or Covenant) we see angels mentioned right at the beginning, even before the birth of Christ. In Luke 1:11–13 we see an angel appearing to Zacharias regarding the birth of John the Baptist. Also, in the same chapter, the same angel Gabriel appears to Mary regarding the birth of Jesus (verses 26–38). An interesting note here is that Zacharias did not believe what Gabriel said and was struck dumb until the birth of John, whereas Mary believed the angel. In verse 34 Mary asked Gabriel how this could happen since she was a virgin, and the angel answers her question very thoroughly. Mary responds in complete faith by saying: *'be it unto me according to thy word'* (verse 38).

This passage in Luke shows that angels can talk to humans and we can talk to angels if one appears. We need to note however that on both these occasions the angel Gabriel had come to Zacharias and Mary according to God's will and not theirs. We do not read that either of them had been praying for such an encounter. Angels appear to us **as God wills** and not as we will. Therefore keep your prayer life fixed on the Lord and not on angels.

When Jesus was preparing for the cross while up on the Mount of Olives He was no doubt feeling the pressure of Calvary coming upon Him, for He said:

> *'Father, if thou be willing, remove this cup from me: nevertheless not my will, but thine, be done.'*
> (Luke 22:42)

We then see how God the Father responds to frail humanity:

> *'And there appeared an angel unto him from heaven, strengthening him.'* (Luke 22:43)

The Lord understands the weakness of our flesh

because He has been through it. I am glad that God the Father dispatches angels to us in times of distress, trauma, major battles etc. What the Father did for His Son Jesus He will do for us as well. Praise the Lord!

Here, the angel is sent to strengthen Him to go through the agonising days ahead. In Matthew 4:11 it says, *'angels came and ministered unto Him.'* In Luke 2:9–14 we see angels declaring the good news along with the brightness of God's glory surrounding them.

During the Great Tribulation we have a most interesting event taking place. An angel preaches the 'everlasting gospel' to the whole world. The reason for this is that only an angel could survive during this time since believers would either die of starvation or have their heads taken off. Also the 144,000 Jewish believers who could not be affected by the Tribulation judgements have been taken into heaven. Therefore, God uses an angel to maintain a gospel witness upon earth for the duration of the seven years until Jesus comes back to fight the battle of Armageddon (Revelation 14:6).

An angel is also used to announce the resurrection of Jesus to Mary Magdalene in John 20:12.

The Bible teaches us that each child has an angel representative in heaven (Matthew 18:10). It is hinted that adult believers do as well (Acts 12:15). As the Psalmist says,

> *'The angel of the Lord encampeth round about them that fear him, and delivereth them.'*　　(Psalm 34:7)

This verse reveals our own personal responsibility to maintain a right relationship with God to ensure angelic protection at all times. That is why we need to stay close to God in prayer and study of His Word, obedient to what He says, submitting to our local leadership and repenting of all known (revealed) sin. That is 'fearing' God and then we can be confident at all times that our wonderful Father in Heaven has His mighty angels around us to deliver us from all evil.

I am sure that the angels that are sent to minister to and for us are much busier than we think since almost all of their activity takes place in the Spirit realm.

The Nature and Vocation of Angels

All angels are sexless (Matthew 22:30). However, they are addressed in the masculine gender and always appear so in Scripture.

In the Day of Judgement angels will stand as witnesses (Luke 12:8–9) to the good and bad. Angels express joy over sinners on earth repenting and coming to the Lord (Luke 15:7). They also conduct dying believers into the presence of God (Luke 16:22). They were the first to announce the gospel to the Gentiles, to Cornelius (Acts 10:1–8). Although angels are seen in Scripture demonstrating awesome power over mankind and the elements, they **do not have power** to separate man from God (Romans 8:38–39).

In 1 Corinthians 13:1 we are informed by Paul that angels have their own language which we are sometimes able to speak by the Holy Spirit. This verse suggests that angels can talk to each other in their angelic language. Angels are definitely not to be worshipped (Colossians 2:18; Revelation 22:8–9). Note the angel refuses to be worshipped or bowed down to but says: *'Worship God.'* Verse 9 here tells us that the angel refers to John as his *'fellow servant.'*

The word of angels is steadfast (firm or sure – Hebrews

2:2). However, through the new birth in Jesus Christ, **man has definitely excelled angels** (Hebrews 2:6–10) since the angels desire to look into redemption but cannot (1 Peter 1:12).

The following chart helps us to understand the rank of authority of all spiritual beings:

God the Father	
God the Son	(John 4:24; 1 John 5:7)
God the Holy Spirit	
Believers in Christ	(2 Corinthians 5:17; Romans 5:17; 1 Corinthians 6:3; Ephesians 2:6; 1 John 4:17 etc.)
Angels (different ranks)	
Unbelievers	(Hebrews 2:7)
Demons	(Luke 10:17–20)

Angels are innumerable (Hebrews 12:22) as John declares in Revelation 5:11:

> '*And I beheld, and I heard the voice of many angels round about the throne and the beasts and the elders: and the number of them was ten thousand times ten thousand, and thousands of thousands.*'

I am a mathematician and ten thousand times ten thousand is a hundred million, besides the thousands of thousands. Consequently, there are a lot of angels. Praise the Lord!

Another characteristic of angels is that they have powers to reveal the future (Revelation 1:1). Also, during the Great Tribulation period, it will be angels who will be the instruments used by God to execute His wrath against rebellious mankind (Revelation 7:1–3 and 8:1–5).

A very interesting event involving angels is also mentioned in the book of Revelation:

> *'And there was war in heaven: Michael and his angels fought against the dragon; and the dragon fought and his angels, and prevailed not; neither was their place found any more in heaven.'*   (Revelation 12:7–8)

I used to think that this event was referring to Satan's initial fall from heaven (Ezekiel 28; Isaiah 14). However, I have come to realise that Revelation 12:7–9 is yet to happen, since Satan is still permitted to accuse the brethren before the throne. However, after this 'war', the devil will never again have access to the throne to accuse believers. Satan's only domain will be earth, and for three and a half years there will literally be hell on earth as he unleashes his final fling on mankind. I am glad I will have been raptured well before!

Chapter 3

Angels on Assignment!

Having given a careful and quite thorough account of angels in the Bible I now want to relay my own experience of angelic encounters.

It was during my second pastorate in Salford, Manchester when an elderly gentleman used to come up to me most Sundays after I had preached and say 'I saw angels around you again this morning, pastor.' When he first began to say this to me I was quite shocked. I had never seen these angels that he was talking about. He was a godly man and had once told me that the Lord had called him to the ministry as a young man but he refused the call. In the two years this continued, I can honestly say that I never once saw an angel.

Some time later, I was asked to go to a college to speak to a group of psychology students. I accepted the offer and talked for two hours about Jesus Christ! I told the students that God spoke to me from time to time and they asked me if He had said anything to me about them. As it happened, God had spoken to me in my quiet time that morning that I would have to pray for one of the class that day. I told them this and waited for the outcome. At the end of the class all the students departed leaving me alone with the teacher. She told me that she was the one I should pray for.

She took me into her office and told me her story. This was certainly a Divine Appointment I shall never forget! The evening before she had planned to commit suicide. The only reason that she did not was my visit the following day. She did not want to cause me any problems. God was in all of this. I shared Jesus with her and she was born again and later received the baptism in the Holy Spirit. She became a radiant soul-winner. To God be the glory. Anyway, one day at our church she told me that she could see a bright light shining around me, just like the older gentleman previously. The Bible says that

> *'at the mouth of two or three witnesses every word shall be established.'*   (2 Corinthians 13:1)

There have been other instances when people have reported angels around me while I was preaching the gospel of Christ.

The Lord Himself

A number of years ago I was going through an enormous trial in my life and every day just seemed as though I was losing the battle. On the Saturday night, I was feeling so low that I did not think I could preach the following day. This has only ever happened to me once. God spoke to me very clearly and said: 'Every time you preach my Word, I send two strong angels to stand by your side. However, I am not sending my angels tomorrow.' There was a pause. I was in shock. The Lord then spoke to me and said, 'I am sending my Son to stand with you tomorrow instead of the angels.'

That gave me strength to come through one of the greatest battles of my life and has stood me in good stead ever since. Thank God for angels. But thank the Father even more for Jesus Christ!

The Spirit Realm

Many years ago I read a book by a very well known preacher and he told how he saw into the spirit realm regularly through visions of angels, demons and the Lord Himself. After reading this I remember praying and asking the Lord to allow me to see into the spirit realm to enable me to be a more effective warrior. It is one thing to pray by faith which we must all do, but it certainly helps if we can see what we are doing as well.

I had been in full-time Christian ministry for 10 years. I had fasted most weeks during that time for up to three days a week. I had prayed in the Spirit for long periods and I can honestly say that I never saw into the spirit realm during those 10 years. Then, it all started. My prayer was answered but not in quite the way I had thought. You will have to be patient and wait for the chapter on demons at this point. (Whenever we talk about the spirit realm we are talking about angels and demons of course.)

In the last five years I have seen angels and demons 'in the spirit' – i.e. in vision form, on many occasions. They are real beings doing a real job.

Angels in Israel

In November of 1995 I went on a special mission to Israel. I have been travelling abroad on such missions since October 1993 and have visited some 18 countries.

On the second day in Israel I was just resting in my bedroom when I saw three angels standing on guard against the wall. I saw them in vision form and throughout my visit to Israel these three angels accompanied me.

I am getting quite used to seeing such phenomena on my missionary trips abroad, particularly when I am involved in intercession for that nation. On a recent trip to Berlin I saw two angels with me on the plane and then again with swords in their hands during spiritual warfare over Germany.

When we read about angels in the Bible they are described as being of different sizes. When I was in New York I spent about three days praying in my hotel room before preaching. During that time I saw a huge angel standing over the area of Jamaica in the Queens district of New York. He had what looked like a threshing instrument in his hand. When I told this to the church, the pastor of the church erupted with excitement because he had seen it also!

I personally believe that angels are all over the place protecting believers, answering our prayers, fulfilling God's purposes etc. The only reason that I now see these things is because I asked.

'Ask and ye shall receive, that your joy may be full.'
(John 16:24)

The most graphic experience of angels was in Paris. Along with an intercessor I had just prayed over the Eiffel Tower for France to experience revival. After we had prayed I saw a vision of heaven open. Angels came down from heaven and occupied the Tower. They all had smiles on their faces. Praise God.

Angels in the Bedroom

At the beginning of 1995 we had a visit from my pastor who came and spoke at our church. During the Sunday service one of our members saw what he described as an angel come into the meeting and sing with us. On the Sunday evening I was in bed wide awake and just going over in my mind what had happened during the day. My wife Ruth was fast asleep. All of a sudden a being appeared in the room on Ruth's side of the bed. I was absolutely stunned! This was not a vision. I could actually see this being with my eyes. I was not sure to start with if it was an angel or a demon. It stood about seven to eight feet tall watching over us. I tried to wake Ruth but she was fast asleep. All sorts of questions were going through my mind! I was just about to speak to it when it vanished into thin air. Then all my questions as to whether it was an angel or a demon went because the room was filled with waves of glory sweeping over my soul for about 20 minutes. I knew that it was an angel of the Lord. He had stood over us for about two and a half minutes, but never spoke a word. That was in January 1995.

Then in April 1995 an angel appeared at the foot of the bed on my side. This time he was shorter that the first one. I leapt up out of the bed towards him to ask him some questions but as soon as I rose up he was gone. Again the awesome presence of God's glory filled the room for about 20 minutes.

In July of the same year there were three angels in my bedroom with the one in the middle being taller than the other two. Then, while I was in Tulsa, Oklahoma in October 1995, I saw a large angel quite different than all the rest standing over my bed.

An Entourage of Angels with Jesus

The following experience is one of the most awesome things that has ever happened to me. I was in a prayer meeting with about eight other people including my wife and children. All of a sudden we were all 'drunk' in the Spirit and could not move. If I had managed to stand up I would have fallen over. All of us were the same, including my children.

I then saw a group of angels escorting Jesus Himself along the corridor outside our prayer room. Jesus came up to me and gave me a personal message about my calling and then said goodbye and joined the angels and I saw them ascend back to heaven. After a few minutes we all came out of the heavy anointing and continued our meeting.

I just want to say that in all of my experiences with angels I have never set out to look for an angel. They have simply appeared quite randomly as the Lord willed, and not as I willed. It would not bother me in the slightest if I never saw another angel. My salvation is not based on such experiences but is firmly rooted and grounded in Jesus Christ and my faith in Him alone. As Paul says:

> *'For by grace are ye saved through faith: and that not of yourselves: it is the gift of God.'* (Ephesians 2:8)

Hence, the grace that gave me my salvation is the same as the grace that allows me to see into the spirit realm.

PART TWO

Demons

Chapter 4

Demons
(Devils)

It is interesting to note that the word 'demon' does not appear anywhere in the Bible although the word 'devil' or 'devils' appears often (115 times). Although the translators of the King James Bible have chosen to translate the Greek word *'daimonion'* into 'devil', it would have been much simpler to have used 'demon'. In fact, *Strong's Concordance* says that the word *'daimonion'* literally means 'a daemonic being'.

You may ask yourself why it is necessary to study about demons anyway. My answer to that is simple: any army that goes to war against the enemy without having any knowledge of who it is fighting is **foolish**.

Paul the apostle says,

> *'Lest Satan should get an advantage of us: for we are not ignorant of his devices.'*   (2 Corinthians 1:11)

We need to learn the devil's devices in order both to defend against his attacks and also to attack when commanded to.

I have been a chess player since a child and was taught early that the best form of defence in a game of chess was to attack. The reason being that when you launch a successful attack it always causes your opponent to defend, thus stopping his attack. The body of Christ has been far too defence-minded. It is time that we did what Jesus said in Matthew 11:12:

> '... *the kingdom of heaven suffereth violence, and the violent take it by force.*'

The Origin of Demons

The Bible tells us where Satan and all his demons come from in Isaiah 14 and Ezekiel 28:

> '*How art thou fallen from heaven, O Lucifer, son of the morning! How art thou cut down to the ground, which didst weaken the nations! For thou hast said in thine heart, I will ascend into heaven, I will exalt my throne above the stars of God: I will sit also upon the mount of the congregation, in the sides of the north: I will ascend above the heights of the clouds; I will be like the most High. Yet thou shalt be brought down to hell, to the sides of the pit.*' (Isaiah 14:12–15)

> '*Son of man, take up a lamentation upon the king of Tyrus, and say unto him, Thus saith the Lord GOD; Thou sealest up the sun, full of wisdom, and perfect in beauty. Thou hast been in Eden the garden of God; every precious stone was thy covering, the sardius, topaz, and the diamond, the beryl, the onyx, and the jasper, the sapphire, the emerald, and the carbuncle, and gold: the workmanship of thy tabrets and of thy*

pipes was prepared in thee in the day that thou wast created. Thou art the anointed cherub that covereth; and I have set thee so: thou wast upon the holy mountain of God; thou hast walked up and down in the midst of the stones of fire. Thou wast perfect in thy ways from the day that thou wast created, till iniquity was found in thee. By the multitude of thy merchandise they have filled the midst of thee with violence, and thou hast sinned: therefore I will cast thee as profane out of the mountain of God: and I will destroy thee, O covering cherub, from the midst of the stones of fire. Thine heart was lifted up because of thy beauty, thou hast corrupted thy wisdom by reason of thy brightness: I will cast thee to the ground, I will lay thee before kings, that they may behold thee.' (Ezekiel 28:12–17)

These portions of Scripture speak for themselves regarding the general fall of Satan from heaven. In Revelation 12:4 it says that the great red dragon drew a third part of the stars of heaven with his tail. This is the Scripture that is used to conclude that a third part of heaven was driven out with Satan. Thus there are two thirds of angels left behind. Consequently, there are twice as many angels as demons. Hallelujah!

However, the Bible itself does not give any graphic description of how evil spirits actually came into being on the earth. Even Peter can only give us a brief glimpse into this matter:

'For if God spared not the angels that sinned, but cast them down to hell, and delivered them into chains of darkness, to be reserved unto judgement . . . '

(2 Peter 2:4)

We have a very interesting reference to the Book of Enoch in Jude verses 13 and 14 regarding evil beings. However, it must be noted that the Book of Enoch is not a recognised book as contained in the canon of Scripture. In other words, we cannot take it as the inspired word of God like we can the Bible. Having said this, page 42 and 43 of the Book of Enoch record the following:

'Wherefore have ye left the high, holy, and eternal heaven, and lain with women, and defiled yourselves with the daughters of men and taken to yourselves wives, and done like the children of earth, and begotten giants (as your) sons. (4) And though ye were holy, spiritual, living the eternal life, you have defiled yourselves with the blood of women, and have begotten (children) with the blood of flesh, and, as the children of men, have lusted after the flesh and blood as those (also) do who die and perish. (5) Therefore have I given them wives also that they might impregnate them, and beget children by them, that thus nothing might be wanting to them on earth. (6) But you were (formerly) spiritual, living the eternal life, and immortal for all generations of the world. (7) And therefore I have not appointed wives for you; for as for the spiritual ones of the heaven, in heaven is their dwelling. (8) And now, the giants, who are produced from the spirits and flesh, shall be called evil spirits upon the earth, and on the earth shall be their dwelling. (9) Evil spirits have proceeded from their bodies; because they are born from men, (and) from the holy waters is their beginning and primal origin; (they shall be evil spirits on earth and) evil spirits shall they be called. (10) (As for the spirits of heaven, in heaven shall be their dwelling, but as for the spirits of the earth which were born upon the earth, on the earth shall be their dwelling.) (11) And the spirits of the giants afflict, oppress, destroy, attack, do battle, and work destruction on the earth, and cause trouble: they take no food, (but nevertheless hunger) and thirst, and cause offences. (12) And these spirits shall rise up against the children of men and against the women, because they have proceeded (from them).'

See also Genesis 6:2–4.

This description of evil spirits fills in the gaps so to speak and is worthy of careful thought and meditation.

The Function of Demons

Jesus tells us in John 10:10 that,

> *'The thief cometh not, but for to steal, and to kill, and to destroy: I am come that they might have life, and that they might have it more abundantly.'*

Stealing, killing and destroying describes perfectly what the devil and all his demons are doing all the time. Satan has no regard for life or any of God's wonderful creation. If Satan had his way he would no doubt destroy everyone and hasten their fate in hell. However, he only has limited power through lies, deception, and temptation. In other words, demons can only gain control over people with human co-operation. Even non-Christian people have resistance against temptation since God created all human beings with a conscience (Romans 2:13–15).

The Varied Tasks of Specific Demons

Paul the apostle gives us some insight into this in Ephesians 6:12:

> *'For we wrestle not against flesh and blood, but against principalities, against powers, against the rulers of the darkness of this world, against spiritual wickedness in high places.'*

Listing these we have:

1. Principalities (occult, sexual lust, partying, murder, sickness, death, mental illness etc.).
2. Powers (controlling governments, nations, cities, towns and homes).
3. Rulers of the darkness of this world.
4. Spiritual wickedness in high (heavenly) places.

Along with these the Bible also mentions Beelzebub who is referred to as *'the prince of the devils'* or, in other words, Satan's commanding general having authority over all of this evil system.

Here is a short list of evil spirits mentioned in the Bible:

(a) Lying spirit (1 Kings 22:22–23)
(b) Foul spirit (Mark 9:25; Revelation 18:2)
(c) Seducing spirits (1 Timothy 4:1)
(d) Familiar spirits (Leviticus 20:27; Isaiah 8:19; 2 Kings 23:24)
(e) Blind spirit (Matthew 12:22)
(f) Dumb and deaf spirit (Mark 9:25)
(g) Spirit of infirmity (these are manifold) (Luke 13:11)
(h) Jealous spirit (Numbers 5:14, 30)
(i) Legion (i.e. many demons) (Mark 5:9)

Hindering Spirits Against Christians
(1 Thessalonians 2:18)

Satan's evil network influences the whole world at every level of society. However, Christians are **not immune**! The devil has assigned certain demons to weaken, control, tempt, seduce, slow down, cause division etc. These would include religious spirits to suppress the life of the Spirit; anti-soulwinning spirits to try to slow down evangelism; anti-financial support to slow down the impact of the gospel; anti-spiritual growth to quench revival.

This is why Christians need to be alert at all times and red hot for God since the Word says:

> *'Be sober, be vigilant* (watchful)*: because your advers-ary the devil, as a roaring lion, walketh about seeking whom he may devour: Whom resist steadfast in the faith, knowing that the same afflictions are accom-plished in your brethren that are in the world.'*

(1 Peter 5:8–9)

We need to feed our spirit with the Word of God more and more. Prayer and fasting produces sensitivity of spirit to know when the enemy is attacking. Personal evangel-ism causes us to stay close to the Lord and keeps our priorities focused on the most important reason for our existence. Living a life of constant praise and worship to God causes the devil to be confused, particularly when he thought he was gaining ground against you! Keep the garments of praise in place at all times to prevent any *'spirits of heaviness'* from slowing you down. (Isaiah 61:3). It is our job to keep the devil off our backs.

Even though Satan has his wicked cohorts garrisoned against believers, we need constantly to remind ourselves of the complete and absolute victory that is ours in Christ Jesus. Read carefully the following Scriptures:

> *'No weapon that is formed against thee shall prosper; and every tongue that shall rise against thee in judgement thou shalt condemn. This is the heritage of the servants of the LORD, and their righteousness is of me, saith the LORD.'* (Isaiah 54:17)

> *'Ye are of God, little children, and have overcome them* (every spirit, verses 1–3): because **greater is he that is in you, than he that is in the world**.*'* (1 John 4:4)

> *'For whatsoever is born of God overcometh the world: **and this is the victory that overcometh the world, even our faith**.*'* (1 John 5:4)

> *'We know that whosoever is born of God sinneth not; but he that is begotten of God **keepeth himself, and that wicked one toucheth him not**.*'* (1 John 5:18)

> *'But thanks be unto God, which **always causeth us to triumph in Christ** and maketh manifest the **savour of his knowledge by us in every place**.*'*
> (2 Corinthians 2:14)

The whole of the teachings of Jesus in the gospels and the rest of the New Testament assure us that we can walk a life of victory over every temptation, test, trial and direct attack from the enemy.

This victory **does not come from ourselves at all**, but has been given to us through the finished work of the death, burial and resurrection of Jesus Christ. Look at what Paul says regarding Christ's victory over all demons:

*'For **in him dwelleth all the fullness of the Godhead bodily** And ye are complete **in him, which is the head of all principality and power**: in whom also ye are circumcised with the circumcision made without hands, in putting off the body of the sins of the flesh by the circumcision of Christ: Buried with him in baptism, wherein also ye are risen with him through the faith of the operation of God, who hath raised him from the dead. And you, being dead in your sins and the uncircumcision of your flesh, hath he quickened **together with him**, having forgiven you all trespasses; blotting out the handwriting of ordinances that was against us, which was contrary to us, and **took it out of the way, nailing it to his cross: and having spoiled principalities and powers, he made a shew of them openly, triumphing over them in it.'*
(Colossians 2:9–15)

Hallelujah! We are always on the winning side when we choose to stay close to Jesus.

The Destiny of all Evil Spirits

'And the devil that deceived them was cast into the lake of fire and brimstone, where the beast and the false prophet are, and shall be tormented day and night for ever and ever ... And whosoever was not found written in the book of life was cast into the lake of fire.'
(Revelation 20:10, 15)

This includes every demon of whatever type. They shall **never** be allowed to torment anyone else ever for all eternity. Praise God! One person once said that if the devil ever reminded them of their past failures then we should turn the tables on to Satan and remind him of his three-fold failure and defeat:

1. Remind him of when **Jesus rose from the dead** and took all the keys away from him.
2. Remind him of the present when the devil is under our feet (Luke 10:17–20).
3. Remind him of his future, crisping and frying in the lake of fire while we enjoy our eternal home in the New Jerusalem, which is in the New Heaven and the New Earth.

Satan is a defeated foe through Jesus Christ. We are protected from all his assaults through the protection of the **blood of the New Covenant**.

> *'And they* (believers) *overcame him by the **blood of the Lamb*** (our defence), *and by the word of their testimony* (our offensive)*; and they loved not their lives unto the death.'*   (Revelation 12:11)

Chapter 5

Who We Are in Christ

The next two chapters are absolutely vital before we begin to look at our final two sections, namely 'deliverance' and 'spiritual warfare'.

Let me ask you some questions: who are you in Christ? How do you see yourself in the body of Christ? Are you weak or strong? Are you bold or timid? Are you a victim or a victor? Are you above or beneath? Your answers to these questions will determine how successful you are as a Christian, particularly in the area of deliverance and spiritual warfare.

We need to look closely at what Jesus has done for us in the New Covenant and how He sees us now operating in His kingdom. Study the following Scriptures:

> 'Therefore if any man be in Christ, he is a new creature: old things are passed away; behold, **all things are become new**.' (2 Corinthians 5:17)

> 'And **ye are complete in him**, which is the head of all principality and power.' (Colossians 2:10)

> 'For he hath made him to be sin for us, who knew no sin; that we might be made **the righteousness of God in him**.' (2 Corinthians 5:21)

*'Verily I say unto you, among them that are born of women there hath not risen a greater than John the Baptist: notwithstanding, **he that is least in the kingdom of heaven is greater than he.**'* (Matthew 11:11)

*'There is therefore now **no condemnation** to them which are **in Christ Jesus, who walk not after the flesh, but after the Spirit.**'* (Romans 8:1)

*'For we are **his workmanship**, created **in Christ Jesus** unto good works, which God hath before ordained that we should walk in them.'* (Ephesians 2:10)

When God created Adam and Eve, they had uninhibited fellowship with the Lord (Genesis 2). They felt no shame or inferiority in the presence of God. The tempter came and Adam fell through disobeying God's command. This brought immediate shame.

'And they heard the voice of the LORD God walking in the garden in the cool of the day: and Adam and his wife hid themselves from the presence of the LORD God amongst the trees of the garden.' (Genesis 3:8)

Through Adam and Eve's sin they brought on themselves guilt, shame, inferiority, fear, unrighteousness etc. They had lost their **right standing with God**. All confidence was gone. Sin with all of its ugliness had now corrupted their nature and God was forced to remove them from the garden so that they would not live eternally in that state (Genesis 3:22–24). The sinful nature would now be passed down to the whole human race bringing with it all the negative influences of life.

I am glad that the Lord knew about all this long before He created mankind. God knew that Adam would sin and so He planned to send Jesus to the cross even before the foundation of the earth to restore mankind to full fellowship with Himself.

The Lord went right to the cause of all the problems that mankind would inevitably go through: **SIN**. Jesus became the sacrifice for the sin of the whole world so that **righteousness** could be restored. Look closely again at 2 Corinthians 5:21. Jesus takes our sin and **makes us righteous**. 1 John 3:7 says,

> *'Little children, let no man deceive you: he that doeth righteousness is righteous, even as he is righteous.'*

That is an awesome statement and we need to allow the Holy Spirit to reveal this truth to us. The blood of Jesus has cleansed our sin and given us a clear conscience (Hebrews 10:22). Then Jesus has removed the root cause of all our weakness and **given us His very own righteousness**. I trust you are getting excited by this revelation! **You are righteous as Jesus is righteous**.

Examine the following portion of Scripture closely:

> *'Grace and peace be multiplied unto you through the knowledge of God and of Jesus our Lord. According as **his divine power** hath given to us **all things** that pertain unto life and godliness, through the knowledge of him that hath called us to glory and virtue. Whereby are given unto us exceeding great and precious promises: **that by these ye might be partakers of the divine nature**, having escaped the corruption that is in the world through lust.'* (2 Peter 1:2–4)

Hence, we are partakers of God's very nature through Christ. Note that Peter says here that we need to apply

God's word (*exceeding great and precious promises*) to our lives to activate this revelation in our experience. It doesn't just happen. He expects us to meditate in His word and to apply it daily to our lives (James 1:22).

Does this revelation of righteousness mean that we do not sin any more? Not at all. We all have the capacity to sin in word, deed, flesh or mind. As John says,

> *'If we say that we have no sin, we deceive ourselves, and the truth is not in us.'*   (1 John 1:8)

(See verses 9 and 10 also.)

Putting all this together, we need to:

(a) Receive a full and complete revelation of our right-standing with God through Christ.
(b) Repent of any sin that we know.
(c) Maintain a life of holiness and watch out for the subtlety of Satan.
(d) Don't give sin a chance by crucifying the flesh daily (Galatians 5:24).

See yourself as God sees you. Do not listen to the devil's lies about who you are in Christ. Whenever we listen to the lies of the devil it keeps us in bondage. Believe only what God says about you and create a good self-image based on God's word.

In the first epistle of John there is a wonderful phrase used throughout the book relating specifically to who we are in Christ. The phrase is *'as he is'* meaning *'as Jesus is'*. In chapter 1 verse 7 John says,

> *'But if we walk in the light, **as he is in the light**, we have fellowship one with another, and the blood of Jesus Christ his Son cleanseth us from all sin.'*

This verse declares that we should be walking in the light as Jesus is in the light. This can only be realised through being born again, of course. This does not refer to non-Christians. They are still in the darkness. We know through experience, however, that we grow in stages in revealed light but this verse declares that we can and should walk in the same light as Jesus.

The next *'as he is'* statement is 1 John 2:6, which says:

> *'He that saith he abideth **in him** ought himself also so to walk, **even as he walked.'***

What a statement! No wonder Jesus said:

> *'Verily, verily, I say unto you, he that believeth on me, the works that I do shall he do also; and greater works than these shall he do; because I go unto my Father.'*
> (John 14:12)

Jesus expects us to walk in the same power, same faith, same light, same anointing and same **results** as He saw. That is our goal. Set your sights higher. Do not be limited by what you have done so far, or by what others have done. Study the gospels and see how easily the miraculous power of God flowed through Jesus. **Walk as He walked!** God expects big things from us under His anointing and leading.

> *'I can do all things through Christ which strengtheneth me.'* (Philippians 4:13)

In 1 John 3:2 we then read:

*'Beloved, now are we the sons of God, and it doth not appear what we shall be: but we know that, when he shall appear, we shall be like **him**: for we shall see him as he is.'*

I used to think that this verse meant that when we see Him face to face He will change us totally to be like Him. However, I am realising more and more that God wants that likeness to Himself while we are here on earth! When people come into contact with us on this earth it should be just like when people met Jesus. Christ is in us and wants to live through us in full measure to produce huge results on earth. The change happens now on earth. No wonder the Word of God says that we are ambassadors for Christ (2 Corinthians 5:20).

We are actually representing God while on the earth. The more we have a revelation of who we are in Christ the greater our impact as ambassadors.

A word of caution. This truth should not promote pride or ego and we must maintain a humble walk before the Lord at all times. Righteousness produces confidence and boldness but we must always remember that *'without him we can do nothing'* (John 15:5) and to have *'no confidence in the flesh.'*

'God resisteth the proud but gives grace to the humble.'
(1 Peter 5:5)

In 1 John 3:3 it says,

*'And every man that hath this hope in him purifieth himself, **even as he is pure**.'*

Isaiah says:

> *'Come now, and let us reason together, saith the* LORD: *though your sins be as scarlet, they shall be **as white as snow**; though they be red like crimson, they shall be **as wool**.'*　　　　　　　　　　　　　　(Isaiah 1:18)

Only through Christ can we fully understand purity as God Himself. Mary Magdalene was a prostitute whom Jesus had to cast devils out of but she was given the privilege to be the first to be told by the angel about the resurrection of Jesus. Whatever you have done in the flesh, the blood of Christ can cleanse you so completely that the light and purity of God Himself can flow through you to reveal Jesus to a needy world.

As we continue through the first epistle of John we come to the next *'as he is'* phrase in chapter 3:7:

> *'Little children, let no man deceive you: he that doeth righteousness is righteous, **even as he is righteous**.'*

Spend a few moments meditating on this statement.

Now look at 2 Corinthians 5:21:

> *'For he hath made him to be sin for us, who knew no sin; that **we might be made the righteousness of God in him**.'*

Therefore, what the word of God reveals here is that **we are righteous as Jesus is righteous**. That is how the Father sees you. You will never enter deliverance ministry or spiritual warfare without a full revelation of righteousness.

What is Righteousness?

To be righteous means to have a right standing before the
Lord, without any sense of guilt, weakness, inferiority or
condemnation. When we have a true understanding of
righteousness we can then understand the following
Scriptures:

> *'Let us therefore come boldly unto the throne of grace,
> that we may obtain mercy, and find grace to help in the
> time of need.'* (Hebrews 4:16)

> *'The wicked flee when no man pursueth: **but the right-
> eous are bold as a lion.'*** (Proverbs 28:1)

Righteousness produces holy boldness!

This boldness is to approach our Heavenly Father as a
son and joint heir with Christ (Romans 8:14–17). This
revelation of righteousness will change your entire life!
You will think differently, act differently, pray differently
and witness with confidence and conviction.

The world and the devil are always trying to accuse us
or put us down. God wants us to rise up as sons of God
and take our place in combat against the forces of darkness and plunder Satan's territory and see revival and
reformation.

This brings us to the last *'as he is'* phrase in 1 John:

> *'Herein is our love made perfect, that we may have
> boldness in the day of judgement: **because as he is, so
> are we in this world.'*** (1 John 4:17)

This has to be one of the most powerful statements in
the New Testament. As Jesus is, so are **we** in this world:

Jesus is victorious – so are we! (1 Corinthians 15:57; 2 Corinthians 2:14).

Jesus is healed – so are we! (1 Peter 2:24; 3 John 2).

Jesus is all powerful – so are we! (in Him.) (Matthew 28:18–20).

Jesus is anointed – so are we! (1 John 2:20, 27).

Jesus is blessed – so are we! (Ephesians 1:3).

Jesus has perfect peace – so have we! (Isaiah 26:3; Philippians 4:6–7).

Jesus reigns – so do we! (Romans 5:17).

Jesus has no fear – neither do we! (1 John 4:18; 2 Timothy 1:7).

Jesus is in heaven – so are we! (Ephesians 2:6).

Jesus is prosperous – so are we! (3 John 2; Psalm 35:27).

Jesus is a devil-crusher – so are we! (Luke 10:17–20).

Now take a closer look at Romans 5:17:

> *'For if by one man's offence death reigned by one; how much more they which receive abundance of grace and of the gift of righteousness **shall reign in life** by one, Jesus Christ.'*

The phrase *'reign in life'* can equally be translated: *'Reign in life as a king.'* God expects you to be reigning in life, not defeated all the time. Victory is ours by right. **As He is, so are we in this world!** Begin to confess this Scripture daily until the penny drops and you begin to realise the full extent of our redemption and salvation in Christ Jesus.

Chapter 6

The Authority of the Believer

Now that we have laid the foundation of who we are in Christ Jesus, we are able to progress and find out what our authority is as believers.

Authority Given to Mankind

Let us go right back to the beginning of creation, to Genesis 1:28–30:

> *'And God said, Let us make man in our image, after our likeness: and **let them have dominion** over the fish of the sea, and over the fowl of the air, and over the cattle, and over all the earth, and over every creeping thing that creepeth upon the earth. So God created man in his own image, in the image of God created he him; male and female created he them. And God blessed them, and God said unto them, Be fruitful, and multiply, and replenish the earth, and subdue it: and have **dominion** over the fish of the sea, and over the fowl of the air, and **over every living thing that moveth upon the earth.***'

This includes all beings that God created, which means Satan and all his demons as well. In other words, God had placed man on the earth as ruler over Satan. The devil did not waste any time in deceiving Adam and Eve to gain control of this delegated authority (Mark 4:15). Satan wanted authority in the earth over mankind and was not prepared just to sit down and take orders from man.

Authority Stolen by Satan

> *'Now the serpent* (see Revelation 12:9) *was more subtle than any beast of the field which the LORD God had made. And he said unto the woman, Yea, hath God said, Ye shall not eat of every tree of the garden?'*
> (Genesis 3:1)

If you read through the whole of chapter 3 you will read of Satan's victory over Adam and Eve, causing God to have to banish man from the Garden of Eden (verse 24). This deception of Satan led to thousands of years of bondage with only limited light, as Satan tyrannised mankind with his ruthless regime.

I am sure that if Adam and Eve had fully realised the extent of their disobedience, they would not have sinned. Their sin brought sin to the whole of the human race along with sickness, torment, poverty, fear and all the other negative forces.

You will notice as you read through the Old Testament that the casting out of devils is never ever mentioned. Man had lost his authority and consequently had to bow to satanic rule. Thank God for the Old Covenant and for the people of God during this time, although we see the limitations again and again of this first covenant because it only worked on the outward man by laws. Consequently, the children of Israel were constantly falling back into devil worship which grieved God's heart. All this because of Adam's transgression.

I am sure Satan was not prepared for God's master plan!

Authority Demonstrated by Jesus

Even before Jesus was out of the cradle Satan had tried to kill Him several times. The devil must have had an idea that the birth of Jesus posed some sort of a threat to his authority. The devil was in for a surprise!

Up until this time the devil had never really experienced much opposition. It is most interesting that the devil tried a similar tactic as he did in the garden of Eden when Jesus went into the wilderness at the commencement of His ministry. (Read Luke 4:1–13.) Satan actually made an attempt to deceive Jesus into handing over His authority:

> *'And the devil said unto him, All this power will I give thee, and the glory of them: **for that is delivered unto me**; and to whomsoever I will, will I give it. If thou therefore wilt worship me, all shall be thine.'*
>
> (Luke 4:6–7)

The devil then had the first shock!

> *'And Jesus answered and said unto him, Get thee behind me, Satan: for it is written, Thou shalt worship the Lord thy God, and him only shalt thou serve.'*
>
> (Luke 4:8)

Satan then tried a dirty trick to try to get Jesus to kill

Himself by jumping off the pinnacle of the temple (verses 9–11). Jesus saw right through this one and said,

> '*. . . It is said, Thou shalt not tempt the Lord thy God.*'
> (Luke 4:12)

At this the devil left Jesus, no doubt shaking his head and wondering how to get rid of Him. Jesus was posing a serious threat to Satan already and He had not even begun to minister.

Jesus then came to Nazareth and made this glorious announcement:

> '*The Spirit of the Lord is upon me, because he hath anointed me to preach the gospel to the poor; he hath sent me to heal the broken hearted, to preach **deliverance to the captives**, and recovering of sight to the blind, to set at liberty them that are bruised, to preach the acceptable year of the Lord.*' (Luke 4:18–19)

In Luke 4:31–36 we read:

> '*And* (Jesus) *came down to Capernaum, a city of Galilee, and taught them on the Sabbath days. And they were astonished at his doctrine: for his word was with power. And in the synagogue there was a man, which had a spirit of an unclean devil, and cried out with a loud voice, saying, Let us alone; what have we to do with thee, thou Jesus of Nazareth? Art thou come to destroy us? **I know thee who thou art**; the Holy One of God. And Jesus rebuked him, saying, Hold thy peace, and come out of him. And when the devil had thrown him in the midst, he came out of him, and hurt him not. And they were all amazed, and spake among*

themselves, saying, What a word is this! For with authority and power he commandeth . the unclean spirits, and they come out.'

I can just imagine the demons going to Beelzebub, once they had been evicted, saying, 'We have never experienced anything like this! We were totally powerless against the words of Jesus.'

In the same chapter of Luke we read,

'And he arose out of the synagogue, and entered into Simon's house. And Simon's wife's mother was taken with a great fever; and they besought him for her. And he stood over her, and rebuked (i.e. took authority over) *the fever; and it left her; and immediately she arose and ministered unto them. Now when the sun was setting, all they that had any sick with divers diseases brought them unto him; and he laid his hands on every one of them, and healed them. And devils also came out of many, crying out, and saying, Thou art Christ the Son of God. And he, rebuking them, suffered them not to speak: for they knew that he was Christ.'*

(Luke 4:38–41)

You will notice here that Jesus dealt with sickness in exactly the same way as He dealt with demons. He simply rebuked the fever and then the devils, taking authority over them with wonderful results. The reason why Jesus did not differentiate between sickness and demons is because they are both part of Satan's work against mankind.

All the way through the gospels we read how Jesus set the captives free, healed all kinds of sickness, infirmity, disease, pains, fevers and various types of demonisation and oppression. Nothing could stand in the way of Jesus **except people's doubt and unbelief**.

> *'And he did not many mighty works there because of their unbelief.'* (Matthew 13:58)

For over three years Jesus totally humiliated Satan and embarrassed even his strongest demons. Jesus also exercised authority over the weather as it became necessary:

> *'And they came to him, and awoke him, saying, Master, master, we perish. Then he arose, and rebuked the wind and the raging of the water: and they ceased, and there was a calm. And said unto them, Where is your faith? And they being afraid wondered, saying one to another, What manner of man is this! For he commandeth even the winds and water, and they obey him.'* (Luke 8:24–25)

This storm is most interesting particularly in the light of what took place immediately afterwards.

> *'And they arrived at the country of the Gadarenes, which is over against Galilee. And when he went forth to the land, there met him out of the city a certain man, which had devils a long time, and wore no clothes, neither abode in any house, but in the tombs. When he saw Jesus, he cried out, and fell down before him, and with a loud voice said, What have I to do with thee, Jesus, thou Son of God most high? I beseech thee, torment me not. (For he had commanded the unclean spirit to come out of the man. For oftentimes it had caught him: and he was kept bound with chains and in fetters; and he brake the bands, and was driven of the*

devil into the wilderness.) And Jesus asked him, saying, What is thy name? And he said, Legion· because many devils were entered into him.'

(Luke 8:26–30)

The demons eventually left and entered some pigs and we read the outcome of this wonderful deliverance:

*'Then they went out to see what was done; and came to Jesus, and found the man, out of whom the devils were departed, sitting at the feet of Jesus, clothed and **in his right mind**: and they were afraid.'*   (Luke 8:35)

Time and time again through the gospels we read of Jesus exercising authority **all the time, in every place**. Satan realised that nothing was going to stop Jesus and so he looked for a way to stop Him permanently by death. However, this played right into God's master plan to restore authority back to mankind.

Before Jesus went to Calvary He began to share His authority with His disciples.

*'Then he called his twelve disciples together, and gave them power and authority **over all devils, and to cure diseases**.'*   (Luke 9:1)

Jesus then appointed another seventy and sent them away to use His authority and declare the kingdom of God.

'And the seventy returned again with joy, saying, Lord, even the devils are subject unto us through thy name. And he said unto them, I beheld Satan as lightning fall from heaven. Behold, I give unto you power to tread on

> *serpents and scorpions, and **over all the power of the*** *
> **enemy:** and nothing shall by any means hurt you.*
> *Notwithstanding in this rejoice not, that the spirits are*
> *subject unto you; but rather rejoice, because your*
> *names are written in heaven.'*   (Luke 10:17–20)

This is absolutely remarkable. The disciples of Jesus were neither born again or baptised in the Holy Spirit and yet they were given authority over sickness, disease and demons. Even though Jesus knew that these same disciples would shortly desert Him and even deny that they knew Him.

How much more should we as born again, holy living, Word-based, tongue-talking, serious believers be healing the sick, driving out demons, raising the dead and causing absolute havoc in the devil's kingdom every day of our lives.

Permanent Restoration of Authority to the Church

> *'But we speak the wisdom of God in a mystery, even*
> *the hidden wisdom, which God ordained before the*
> *world unto our glory: which none of the princes of*
> *this world knew: for had they known it, **they would not*** *
> **have crucified the Lord of glory.'***
>   (1 Corinthians 2:7–8)

Satan may be the most subtle of all God's creation (Genesis 3:1) through lies and deception, but he was made to look totally stupid at the cross and by the resurrection. All the devil wanted to do was to stop Jesus. He was so intent on killing Jesus that he never once saw what was really taking place.

What Took Place on the Cross?

1. **Jesus took all our sins upon Himself** (Isaiah 53:4–5; 2 Corinthians 5:21). He did this to make us righteous (2 Corinthians 5:21) and to have dominion and authority over sin (Romans 6:12–14) which produces a clear conscience (Hebrews 10:22) and a bold relationship with the Father (Proverbs 28:1; Hebrews 4:16; 1 John 4:17).
2. **Jesus bore all our sickness and disease** (Isaiah 53:4–5 with Matthew 8:17; Psalm 103:2–3; 3 John 2; 1 Peter 2:24; Exodus 15:26). He did this so that we could be healed and walk in total health and bring healing and health to others. God's best for all believers is complete health.
3. **Jesus took our poverty on the cross**. (3 John 2; Galatians 3:13–14; Philippians 4:19; Deuteronomy 8:18; 28:1–15).

    > *'For ye know the grace of our Lord Jesus Christ, that, **though he was rich, yet for your sakes he became poor, that ye through his poverty might be rich.'***　(2 Corinthians 8:9)

4. **Jesus took our fear of death** (Hebrews 2:15).
5. **Jesus took all oppression** (Isaiah 53:7; Acts 10:38).

Jesus Christ the Son of God took upon Himself every negative thing that had come upon mankind. Everything that Adam lost in the garden Jesus has given back to us. The intimacy of relationship that Adam had with God is possible once more through the new birth. Even more so in fact because we are made partakers of God's nature through applying the promises of God in our lives (2 Peter 1:3–4). Adam was not actually born again as we are (or can be). In fact we have all that Adam had in the garden and much more! (See Romans 5 – notice the term *'much more'* repeated again and again.)

Jesus became the sacrificial Lamb, to make atonement for the sins of the whole world (1 John 2:2). While Jesus was on the cross He made this statement:

> *'And when Jesus had cried with a loud voice, he said, Father, into thy hands I commend my spirit: and having said this, he gave up the ghost.'* (Luke 23:46)

As He died, therefore, His spirit went directly to His Father in heaven. We also know that His body was laid in a tomb (Luke 23:50–53). But what about His soul?

Where did the soul of Jesus go to after He died? We will now examine carefully what Luke tells us in the Acts of the Apostles:

> *'For David speaketh concerning him, I foresaw the Lord always before my face, for he is on my right hand, that I should not be moved: Therefore did my heart rejoice, and my tongue was glad; moreover also my flesh shall rest in hope: **because thou wilt not leave my soul in hell**, neither wilt thou suffer thine Holy One to see corruption. Thou hast made known to me the ways of life; thou shalt make me full of joy with thy countenance. Men and brethren, let me freely speak unto you of the patriarch David, that he is both dead and buried, and his sepulchre is with us unto this day. Therefore being a prophet, and knowing that God had sworn with an oath to him, that of the fruit of his loins, according*

> *to the flesh, he would raise up Christ to sit on his throne; he seeing this before spake of the resurrection of Christ, **that his soul was not left in hell**, neither his flesh did see corruption. **This Jesus hath God raised up**, whereof we all are witnesses.'*   (Acts 2:25–32)

Thus the soul of Jesus went into hell for three days and nights (compare Jonah 2:1–9). Read carefully through Psalm 22 and Psalm 88 and look out for these prophetic statements of Jesus' experience in hell:

> *'Many bulls have compassed me: strong bulls of Bashan have beset me round.'*   (Psalm 22:12)

> *'They gaped upon me with their mouths, as a ravening and a roaring lion.'*   (Psalm 22:13)

> *'For my soul is full of troubles: and my life draweth nigh unto the grave.'*   (Psalm 88:3)

> *'Free among the dead, like the slain that lie in the grave, whom thou rememberest no more: and they are cut off from thy hand.'*   (Psalm 88:5)

> *'Thou hast laid me in the lowest pit, in darkness, in the deeps.'*   (Psalm 88:6)

> *'. . . I am shut up, and I cannot come forth.'*
> (Psalm 88:8c)

> *'Wilt thou shew wonders to the dead?'*   (Psalm 88:10a)

> *'They came round about me daily like water; they compassed me about together.'*   (Psalm 88:17)

Jesus went single-handedly into hell itself without His Father or the Holy Spirit or the angels to comfort or strengthen Him. The devil and all his evil hosts must have rejoiced and probably had a party to celebrate their victory over Jesus. Not only had Jesus stopped preaching, healing, teaching and casting out devils, but all of His disciples had deserted Him as well. Just imagine all the imps, cohorts, unclean spirits, powers, rulers of darkness, principalities and every foul spirit saluting Beelzebub and Satan in their greatest achievement so far. Satan's pride must have been fed more than ever. **But** that is **not** the end of the story!

Right in the middle of all this rejoicing Jesus walked up to Satan, after 72 hours have been completed, fulfilling the Scriptures. Jesus took the crown stolen from Adam off Satan's head, and took the keys of death, hell and the grave from the devil. He then spoiled principalities and powers and made an open show of them. (Colossians 2:15). At this point **all the rejoicing stopped. Jesus defeated Satan on His own** and took away all his authority that he had since Adam. Jesus then rose from the dead, taking all of man's authority from Satan.

In Matthew 28 we then read,

> *'And Jesus came and spake unto them, saying, all power* (Greek = authority) *is given unto me in heaven and in earth. Go ye therefore, and teach all nations, baptising them in the name of the Father, and of the Son, and of the Holy Spirit.'*　　(Matthew 28:18–19)

Jesus did not have to die on the cross for His own sin because **He had no sin**. He did it for us. Similarly, He did not need to go into hell to gain authority over Satan since He had already demonstrated His authority for three and a half years. Jesus went into hell therefore to restore authority back to mankind so that we could have authority on the earth to do all that Jesus did.

> *'Verily, verily, I say unto you, he that believeth on me,
> the works that I do shall he do also; and greater works
> than these shall he do; because I go unto my Father.'*
>
> (John 14:12)

Jesus then went to heaven and told His disciples to wait for the Holy Spirit to empower them all. The day of Pentecost came and weak, shy, faithless, timid men like Peter were filled with the Holy Spirit, spoke in tongues and began to exercise the authority of Jesus immediately. Three thousand people were saved on the first day! Authority was now restored to God's people and Satan's nightmare continues. The devil only had to cope with Jesus and a few of His disciples before Calvary. Now he has to face the whole Church walking in the same power and authority as Jesus.

PART THREE

Deliverance

Chapter 7

Setting the Captives Free

'The Spirit of the Lord God is upon me; because the LORD hath anointed me to preach good tidings unto the meek; he hath sent me to bind up the brokenhearted, to proclaim liberty to the captives, and the opening of the prison to them that are bound; to proclaim the acceptable year of the LORD, and the day of vengeance of our God; to comfort all that mourn; to appoint unto them that mourn in Zion, to give unto them beauty for ashes, the oil of joy for mourning, the garment of praise for the spirit of heaviness; that they might be called trees of righteousness, the planting of the LORD, that he might be glorified.' (Isaiah 61:1–3)

In the New Testament Jesus quotes this same verse of Scripture at the beginning of His earthly ministry:

*'The Spirit of the Lord is upon me, because he hath anointed me to preach the gospel to the poor; he hath sent me to heal the brokenhearted, **to preach deliverance to the captives**, and recovering of sight to the blind, **to set at liberty them that are bruised.'***

(Luke 4:18)

Also the first thing that Jesus said in Mark's account of the Great Commission is:

> *'And these things shall follow them that believe; **in my name shall they cast out devils**; they shall speak with new tongues.'*   (Mark 16:17)

It is therefore most interesting to realise what place the ministry of deliverance has in the church if Jesus Himself made mention at the beginning and end of His earthly ministry.

I would like to put a note in at this point and say that if you have picked up this book to learn about the ministry of deliverance and you have skipped the previous sections and come right to this one, then **please go back** and at least read, study and inwardly digest chapters 5 and 6.

This ministry is not for flaky, casual, occasional, sugar-coated, lazy Christians but serious, diligent, Word-based, compassionate overcomers who desire to help mankind through love and patience to the glory of God.

How I Began in Deliverance

In 1980 I found myself pastoring a church in Liverpool, England. I had been thrown in at the deep end at the ripe old age of 21. I knew very little.

I remember going to see my pastor one day and saying, 'Pastor, I am confident about leading people to Christ, I am happy about laying hands on the sick, and praying for people to receive the baptism in the Holy Spirit is not a problem either, **but** I would not have the first idea of what to do if I met demons in people.' I did not know that my pastor had been involved with the ministry of deliverance since 1958! A divine appointment indeed. I later found out how remarkable it was that Aubrey Whittall was my pastor, since very few ministers in that particular denomination knew much about the subject. The Lord arranged for me to meet a top authority on the subject. God does not make any mistakes. The Lord is leading our steps much more closely than we often realise.

> '*A man's heart deviseth his way; but the* LORD *directeth his steps.*'   (Proverbs 16:9)

Aubrey then proceeded to teach me for about 10 weeks (I used to have a morning with him every two weeks) to train me from the Word as well as his many years' experience. It was a tremendous privilege for me to sit at his feet to listen and ask loads of questions. It was the best training I could have had anywhere. Praise God!

The Gift of Discerning of Spirits
(1 Corinthians 12:10)

During the weeks that Aubrey was teaching me about this aspect of the ministry he described to me how the spiritual gifts operated which accompanied this work. He explained about the gift of discerning of spirits. This gift eliminates **guesswork**. With this gift of discerning of spirits you **know** when a particular manifestation or problem is caused by a demon. Sometimes you do not need this gift to know. It is quite often obvious!

If you are a serious believer and are baptised in the Holy Spirit with the evidence of speaking with tongues and you desire to be used by the Lord to set the captives free – if you want this gifting then ask the Lord right now and expect this anointing to come. The Bible tells us to covet spiritual gifts (1 Corinthians 14:1). Also ask Him for 'working of miracles' and 'the word of knowledge' which are used much in this ministry of the miraculous.

Fasting and Prayer

Any thoroughly effective deliverance ministry must be accompanied with **regular** fasting and prayer. Read Isaiah 58 and Matthew 17:21 (King James Version). Notice that the word 'fasting' has been removed or relegated to the margin in most of the modern versions!

I have personally fasted (with much prayer) virtually every week for the past 15 years for between one and a half to three days a week. I have had seasons of fasting where I have fasted for two and a half days every week for a few months. If I am physically tired then I stop fasting! I always drink liquids during all my fasts such as tea, coffee, water and fruit juice.

Sometimes I pray much during the fast and sometimes I just fast and then pray afterwards when I am physically stronger. Do not get bound by rules regarding this wonderful subject. Fasting also keeps you physically in good shape and deals with your appetite!

When Jesus began His earthly ministry what was the very first thing that the Holy Spirit led Him into? It was a 40-day fast! This was before Jesus ever preached, prayed for the sick or performed one miracle. If fasting was necessary for Jesus, then how much more for us. I am convinced that we will never realise our maximum potential in ministry without regular times of prayer and fasting.

In Acts 13:1–3 we read,

> *'Now there were in the church that was at Antioch certain prophets and teachers; as Barnabas, and*

*Simeon that was called Niger, and Lucius of Cyrene, and Manaen, which had been brought up with Herod the tetrarch, and Saul. As they ministered to the Lord, and **fasted**, the Holy Ghost said, Separate me Barnabas and Saul for the work wherewith I have called them. And when they had **fasted** and prayed, and laid their hands on them they sent them away.'*

We see here how fasting was normal for the early church. Fasting here preceded a missionary trip and led to divine guidance as to who should go on this particular trip. It is very interesting to note that the first time that Jesus mentions fasting in the New Testament He says,

*'Moreover **when** ye fast, be not, as the hypocrites, of a sad countenance: for they disfigure their faces, that they appear unto men to fast. Verily I say unto you, They have their reward.'* (Matthew 6:16)

Therefore, Jesus takes it for granted that we will fast. Jesus did not say **if** you fast but **when**! Thus we choose when to fast. Jesus goes on to say about fasting:

'But thou, when thou fastest, anoint thine head, and wash thy face; That thou appear not unto men to fast, but unto thy Father which is in secret: and thy Father, which seeth in secret, shall reward thee openly.' (Matthew 6:17–18)

The Lord has only spoken to me on two occasions regarding fasting and each time it was to do a longer fast than normal because of major changes in my life. One was a three and a half day total fast with just water. The other

71

was a 21-day partial fast with just some toast in the evening plus drinks. The latter fast was just before we embarked on pioneering a new church and ministry called Life Changing Ministries. I can now see why the Lord wanted me to go on such a fast in preparation for what I am doing now. I never imagined for one moment that I would be travelling all over the world teaching, preaching, praying for the sick and casting out devils in such a short time. I have been to 18 countries in the last two and a half years with many more planned. It pays to obey the Spirit of the Lord every time He speaks!

What Does Fasting Do?

Fasting helps you to tune in to the voice of The Lord. It helps us to become more sensitive to His voice. When a radio is not quite tuned in properly you can often hear several channels all at once but none clearly. You then have to tune in to the right wavelength to hear the correct voice. So it is in the Spirit realm. There are many voices trying to speak to us but only one voice is profitable to listen to. That is the voice of The Lord Himself. Job says:

> *'For God speaketh once, yea twice, yet man perceiveth it not.'* (Job 33:14)

The problem isn't with God not speaking but with us not being in the place where we can hear His voice. When it comes to the ministry of deliverance you have to hear God speaking regularly or you will never be successful, particularly with strong cases. The gifts of the Spirit play a vital part in this area of ministry.

Personal Purity and Holiness

> *'Who shall ascend into the hill of the LORD? or who shall stand in his holy place? He that hath clean hands, and a pure heart; who hath not lifted up his soul unto vanity, nor sworn deceitfully. He shall receive the blessing from the LORD, and righteousness from the God of his salvation.'*
> (Psalm 24:3–5)

> *'Having therefore these promises, dearly beloved, let us cleanse ourselves from all filthiness of the flesh and spirit, perfecting holiness in the fear of God.'*
> (2 Corinthians 7:1)

We need to walk in holiness and purity at all times in any area of ministry to experience the full anointing of God upon our lives. This is so important in the area of deliverance because the demons know what our standing is spiritually!

> *'Then certain of the vagabond Jews, exorcists, took upon them to call over them which had evil spirits the name of the Lord Jesus, saying, We adjure you by Jesus whom Paul preacheth. And there were seven sons of one Sceva, a Jew, and chief of the priests, which did so. And the evil spirit answered and said, Jesus I know, and Paul I know; but who are ye? And the man in whom the evil spirit was leaped on them, and overcame them, and prevailed against them, so that they fled out of that house naked and wounded.'*
> (Acts 19:13–15)

It is important that we repent of all known sin in our lives before ministering to others. Solomon says:

> *'They made me the keeper of the vineyards; but mine own vineyard have I not kept.'*
>
> (Song of Solomon 1:6)

Paul says:

> *'But I keep under my body, and bring it into subjection: lest that by any means, when I have preached to others, I myself should be a castaway.'*
>
> (1 Corinthians 9:27)

We have to make sure in any aspect of ministry that our own walk with the Lord is right before we minister into the lives of others. You can only go on for a short time in ministry before you have to come aside from people and seek Him afresh. Anyone can 'dry up' spiritually. You are ultimately responsible for watching over your own life. Seek God regularly and you will see an increased anointing in your life in this area of ministry. Never be content with where you are; always press on for more anointing through your life to help hurting humanity.

Different Levels of Bondage

When we first begin ministering deliverance The Lord usually breaks us in gently to start with. I can remember my first deliverance case as a young pastor of 21 years old. A lady shared with me how she had terrible headaches every month. It caused her such distress that she had to have one or two days off work every month because of it. She asked me to pray for her. We talked for a while and it transpired that she had backslidden a number of years earlier and during that time had a nasty fall hurting her head. The Lord showed me that a demon spirit was causing the problem and I cast out the spirit in Jesus' Name and she was completely delivered to the Glory of God!

This really encouraged me and strengthened my faith and belief in deliverance. It also made me wonder how many people there were in the body of Christ with similar problems that also needed this kind of simple deliverance. After 15 years of deliverance ministry I can tell you that many people have needed deliverance at this simple level. The Lord always moves us on in any avenue of ministry.

As the months passed in my pastoral office I found myself ministering along similar lines on many occasions. However, I found that as I progressed with 'small' cases along would come a much harder case. Every time this happened I would have to draw close to God even more with fasting and prayer. Up to this point I found that the 'troublemakers' would leave quite easily at my rebuke in the Name of Jesus Christ. One day I was ministering to a person and the spirit would not leave until I found out its name. I have discovered that some demons will not leave without you knowing their name and then commanding them to leave by that name.

Notice how Jesus deals with Legion:

> *'For he said unto him, Come out of the man, thou unclean spirit. And he asked him, What is thy name? And he answered, saying, My name is Legion: for we are many.'*   (Mark 5:8–9)

The demons did not come out this time when Jesus said 'Come out'. Instead they left after He had determined their name.

How to Obtain the Names of Stubborn Spirits

Sometimes you can come up against a 'blockage' while you are ministering to someone being delivered of smaller spirits. This can be because of a need for repentance from unforgiveness or unbelief. Or it can be because you need the name of a stronger demon. The best way to deal with this is to **stop ministering** and pray in the spirit. Ask the person being ministered to if they have received a name. Often they will have, and can give it to you. Other times they will get nothing and you will have to pray in tongues until you get the name. I have done this hundreds of times and it is awesome to see the accuracy of the word of knowledge in operation. Sometimes, as soon as you mention the name, the person goes wild! I have had some demons talk to me and even threaten me, while others just leave after a rebuke. Either way they have to leave.

Groups of Spirits

Once you get into the flow of deliverance ministry you will notice certain patterns forming. One of them is that demons usually come out in groups of similar spirits. For example, if the person has been sexually abused there are often different sexual demons to cast out, such as lust, fornication, adultery, an unclean spirit, etc. Another example would be if a person had been severely rejected by someone and they held a major grudge as a result. In this case the person needs to forgive from the heart and then ask if resentment, bitterness, hate or even a desire to murder is troubling them. I have seen this many times. Unforgiveness leads to resentment which leads to bitterness which turns into hate and can ultimately lead to murder. If ever someone tells you any of this list of problems then ask the person where it came from. You will always trace it back to unforgiveness. Notice the warning given to us about a root of bitterness in Hebrews 12:15 and Ephesians 4:31.

People who have been bound by such problems as resentment or bitterness need a **revelation of love**. Once you have a full revelation of love (*agape*) you will never again fall into the devil's trap of getting offended, bearing grudges, hating or any of those negative emotions. So what is love?

> *'Love suffereth long, and is kind; love envieth not; love vaunteth* (boasts) *not itself, is not puffed up. Doth not behave itself unseemly, seeketh not her own, is not easily provoked, thinketh no evil; Rejoiceth not in iniquity, but rejoiceth in the truth; Beareth all things, believeth all things, hopeth all things, endureth all things. **Love never fails.**'* (1 Corinthians 13:4–8)

If you still struggle in the area of unforgiveness, resentment, bitterness or hate then pray now this prayer with all your heart:

> Dear Heavenly Father, I come to you recognising my need of love. I pray in faith for this love and believe that I receive your agape love deep into my heart right now in the Name of Jesus Christ. Amen.

Set yourself the goal that any time a person hurts you, talks about you, slanders you or rejects you, that it will become like water off a duck's back to you. You will just simply smile at the situation and lovingly bless the people and carry on. You cannot afford to carry these negative emotions around with you and ruin your testimony. **You can overcome**. I have to walk in love all the time as a preacher. People speak against me all the time. God spoke to me once about this and what He said should really encourage you. I was going through so much persecution of this kind a few years ago, and people were saying all kinds of evil against me. Then the Lord said this to my heart: 'Every time anyone speaks against you I will take the anointing off their lives and give it to you!' **Hallelujah! No wonder the word tells us to rejoice when we are persecuted for righteousness' sake.**

Jesus said,

> *'Blessed are they which are persecuted for righteousness' sake: for theirs is the kingdom of heaven. Blessed are ye, when men shall revile you, and persecute you, and shall say all manner of evil against you falsely, for my sake. Rejoice, and be **exceeding glad**: for great is your reward in heaven: for so persecuted they the prophets which were before you.'*   (Matthew 5:10–12)

Can Demons Return to the Same Person?

Many people ask this question in the light of what Jesus said in the following passage:

> *'When the unclean spirit is gone out of a man, he walketh through dry places, seeking rest; and finding none, he saith, I will return unto my house whence I came out. And when he cometh, he findeth it swept and garnished. Then goeth he, and taketh to him seven other spirits more wicked than himself: and they enter in, and dwell there: and the last state of that man is worse than the first.'*   (Luke 11:24–26)

(See also Matthew 12:43–45.)

If this were the only passage of Scripture on deliverance in the Bible then we must never cast devils out of anybody. The consequences would be disastrous! However, Jesus said to us:

> *'And these signs shall follow them that believe; In my name shall they cast out devils; they shall speak with new tongues.'* (Mark 16:17)

So how do we understand Luke 11:24–26? Look closely at 2 Peter 2:20–22. This gives us the answer quite plainly. Those people who backslide open themselves up to evil spirits. Those Christians who go on with the Lord, read the word, pray, fellowship, witness etc. **cannot** be overcome by the powers of darkness. We are protected by the blood of Jesus. Demons cannot gain entry into a Christian's life unless they backslide and get involved with sin. Therefore, once you have been delivered of a spirit, it has no legal right to enter again. Praise God!

I believe that Jesus was talking to unsaved, unprotected people in Luke 11:24–26 or backsliders. This gives us confidence to minister to Christians who need deliverance and want to go on with the Lord. I personally believe that we should not therefore minister deliverance to unsaved people or else they will attract seven stronger demons back into them. I would lead such a person to Christ and then cast the devils out of them. The only exception to this in my life, was when I was once asked to visit someone.

I was greeted at the door by a man who was obviously severely bound by the powers of darkness. I talked to him for a while and it turned out that his parents and grandparents were Satanist high priests. This poor man wanted desperately to be free. I talked to him about Jesus and how to become a Christian. He said that he had tried but could not say the prayer. Now, because he wanted to know Jesus, I began to minister deliverance to him to free him enough to get saved. That is exactly what happened. I cast out every thing I could think of and he was thrown all over the place to start with. Then he was slain in the spirit and I proceeded to minister to him. After about an hour of much deliverance I was able to lead him to Christ. I then cast out many more demons and eventually prayed for him to be filled with the Holy Spirit. I learnt much that day and believe that it was a divine appointment for both him and me. The Lord has done that many times with me to teach and to train me.

Every so often I will find myself faced with a really difficult case. I always adopt the same approach with each new case. We always use a basic deliverance questionnaire which helps us greatly to get started. Then the word of knowledge sorts out the rest.

Deliverance Questionnaire

If you would like copies of the deliverance questionnaire simply write to our office address at the back of this book.

Chapter 8

Case Studies of Deliverance

Case 1: Myself

When I first became a Christian I had a very dramatic conversion. I was 19 years old when I surrendered my life to Jesus. I had been involved in rock music, drinking, smoking, discos etc. I started going to church, reading my Bible and developing a tremendous hunger for God, His word and everything to do with Christianity. I was baptised in water, then I was baptised in the Holy Spirit with the evidence of speaking in tongues. The Lord then called me into full-time ministry and within 18 months of being saved I was pastoring my first church at the age of 21. However, as I began learning about the ministry, counselling etc., I realised that my mind was troubled constantly. I did not know what it was at the time. I had already been delivered from smoking and alcohol and had a single-minded desire to serve the Lord for the rest of my life. But my mind was troubled constantly. I did not know what a sound mind was according to 2 Timothy 1:6–7. I began regular fasting and prayer, filling my mind with the Word of God and growing in my understanding of authority all the time. It took about 12 months for my mind to be clear of what I now believe to be demonic disturbance. Over the years I have practised self-deliverance whenever I have been aware of anything troubling me. I can do this because I have all authority over the powers of darkness. (See Luke 10:17–20.)

There was an occasion many years ago when I asked my pastor to pray for me and I was delivered instantly. It is always good to have someone to pray for you, if you need to, who is moving in a greater level of revealed authority than you are. Therefore, once you know who you are in Christ Jesus and you know by God's Word that you have **His** authority then you can practise self-deliverance. Then if you need further help ask someone with greater authority than you to finish it off. However, don't wear other people out. Look what the Word says:

> *'Submit yourselves therefore to God. **Resist** the devil, and he will flee from **you**.'* (James 4:7)

As you mature in Christ you will find that you can cast the devil out in Jesus name. If you are involved in ministering deliverance to others then teach the people this principle so that they grow up and you don't wear out! We can keep people's faith small by restricting them. We should be always seeking to release people into their God-given ministries. You will find that as they grow, so you will grow also. Then God can lead you into a higher calling. Delegate or stagnate!

I find now in my own life and spiritual walk that there is complete peace in my mind, emotions, body and soul. I find that the enemy attacks me from without rather than from within now, and when he does I have to rebuke him and cast him away. For instance, from time to time he will try to lay symptoms of sickness on my body. I know my covenant with God and so I resist all sickness, disease or infirmity from my body and I soon get the victory. If the symptoms persist then I get all the healing Scriptures out and preach against the attack until victory comes. I have been doing this now for about 16 years and can testify that my body is in total health and I have not needed a doctor in all that time. To God be the glory!

The other kind of attack is in the mind. The devil tries to play tricks on your mind from time to time: for example with lies, deception, or false accusation. You have to deal with such attacks quickly in the name of Jesus or they will begin to take root and bring discouragement which leads to depression. Do not listen to the devil's lies. Speak God's word to the lies. His word is **truth**! This is really called spiritual warfare which will be dealt with in Part Four. Thus we see that deliverance is **permanent**. Once you have been delivered and you continue to go on with the Lord then you stay free for the rest of your life.

Case 2: My Wife

When I married Ruth she was a very shy, reserved person with a tremendous capacity to serve. She was saved and baptised in the Holy Spirit. As soon as we were married we started a family. In fact David was born 9 months after we were married. Joy arrived 12 months later. It seemed like all we ever did in those early years was change nappies and prepare baby food. I was out ministering much of the time and Ruth was in the flat looking after the babies. I had much more opportunity to grow in spiritual things than Ruth as a result. I surged ahead spiritually as I pastored the church, and I realised that Ruth was not growing as I was. I never thought that Ruth needed major deliverance. Every time that God would speak to me she would attack me verbally. I could not understand this and tried to explain gently to her. As time passed by we changed churches as the Lord instructed me. Every time we moved Ruth would attack me vehemently. I felt quite alone having to carry this responsibility all on my own but knew that I was hearing from God. I was growing all the time in the spiritual gifts, healing, miracles and so on. When we began Life-Changing Ministries in Stoke-on-Trent in 1991 the deliverance ministry that was upon my life began to grow. God kept sending us tough cases to deal with and we were learning more and more all the time. One day Ruth came to me and said to me that she thought that she needed deliverance. I had never really thought too much about the likelihood of this. I said that I would put her through a test to see if she needed any deliverance. She had been through the questionnaire a few years earlier but nothing much had changed. Was I in for a shock!

We talked for a while and she shared how she felt her upbringing had left her crushed, inferior and having a very poor self-image. Ruth knows the Scriptures on who she is in Christ but still had these overwhelming forces controlling her. We began to pray and all kinds of things started to leave her. Religious spirits, anti-Semitism, unbelief, Nazi spirits, resentment, Roman spirits, Freemasonry, victim of Jezebel, control etc. Ruth has since had about 20 sessions of ministry with me and she is a totally different person. She used to think that it was her personality to be the way she was. The fruit of the Spirit is now growing like never before and her ministry is taking off. In fact it was during this time of deliverance that Jesus called her into the fivefold ministry. I believe her deliverance has released her call. She now pastors the church while I travel to the nations and she loves it. She is totally different from the woman I married 15 years ago.

I believe that these little troublemakers are there to stop the fruit and gifts of the Spirit from growing in our lives. If you are not developing in any or all of the fruit mentioned in Galatians 5:22–23 then it could be that you need deliverance. Usually the people that oppose this ministry the most, are the very ones who need it the most! So be careful – never be too proud to ask a competent minister to pray with you, and make sure that you are completely free to serve God. I do not look for demons. I do not need to. I was preaching in a town in England one day to a packed church that was not used to deliverance ministry. I had no intention of ministering deliverance. As soon as I came to the end of my message a girl on the front row began screaming. Then a man fell down under the power of the Spirit and began manifesting on the floor. I ministered to them and a number of other people were also set free that day.

Case 3: A Rape Victim

I was preaching in Northern Ireland for a weekend a few years ago. On the Sunday evening the service began at 6:00 pm and the church was pretty full. Wonderful things happened by the grace of God. People were healed, delivered, saved and baptised in the Holy Spirit. The meeting went on for quite a while and a large proportion of it was ministry time. At 11:45 pm most of the people had left apart from about six of us. There was a young lady at the back of the building sobbing her heart out, with another lady beside her trying to comfort her. I was very tired and all I wanted to do was to get to bed since I had an early flight the next morning. I asked what the matter was but the young lady would not speak to me. Eventually she shared her story with one of the female youth leaders. She was 21 years old at the time but on her eighteenth birthday had been raped. She had not been able to look at a man or even talk to one since. I asked her if I could pray with her. In just a few seconds she was totally free. She threw her arms around me with joy at her new-found freedom. She was delivered from that evil spirit that had tormented her for three years. This case shows that some people can be set free from things quickly without any fuss or manifestations. Every case is different.

Case 4: Major Hereditary Curses

One day a lady called 'Jane' (I have changed her name for confidentiality) walked into our church for the first time and I noticed that she joined the prayer line for deliverance. When I prayed for her she manifested demons and I could see that she needed a lot of help. I asked one of our team to go through the sheet (deliverance questionnaire) with Jane and it did not reveal much. The sheet usually gives some sort of idea how much bondage there is and often the level of bondage. Not in this case. Jane had been a Christian for about 25 years and speaking with tongues for many years. She had always known that she needed deliverance and had been seeking it for a long time. All the usual reasons for bondage were checked and very little showed up. She had had a good upbringing and had not been involved in any major sin or occult. Yet there were severe problems.

After a few weeks my wife and I spent some time with Jane since nothing was happening. It took a long time before anything started. I had never met anything like this before. One of the first major breakthroughs came when

Jane admitted holding deep resentment towards God for the way she was. She was in constant emotional turmoil. After a few sessions of prayer and a little progress I had a vision of a big black spider's web with a black widow spider at the centre. I took authority over it and it went wild. We prayed against everything that the Holy Spirit showed me at each session. After many months Jane said to me that she did not feel that she was getting anywhere. I kept on encouraging her to keep believing, speaking the Word, fasting and praying and all the usual things. Then one day I remember seeing in vision form what looked to me like a huge pizza covering the spider's web. Each time we had prayer with her over the next few months I saw this pizza go one piece at a time. There were all kinds of spirits that were intertwined at each session and it did seem a very slow process. Every time I would pray with her I would have this vision which I shared with her each time: that more was going. Eventually I saw this pizza finally go and all I could see was the spider's web. At each session the web went a bit at a time. I was determined to see this through to the end for Jane's sake. She had suffered such torment. Freedom was her inheritance and I was responsible for helping her through.

As the months turned into years Jane began to testify that she was beginning to sense freedom coming slowly. Praise God! It transpired that a few generations ago a human sacrifice had been made and Jane was the victim of that act. Or one of the victims!

During the years that I have been involved with this case I must have named and cast out at least two thousand demons of varying sizes. Some came out in groups. At one time with Jane we seemed to be getting nowhere. The Holy Spirit showed us a multi-headed cobra with the names of about 20 fears. I got Jane to renounce each fear individually since it would not come out in one. (Incidentally, fear had been a major part of her life.) As each fear was named it screamed out. Many spirits would manifest by coughing or yawning.

One of the outward evidences that a person is coming to freedom is the face. Jane's face looks so different now. In fact I always look at a person's face after deliverance and you can usually see a difference with the vast majority of people. I know ministers who have admitted that they never get involved with deliverance. I have learnt so much through this case and others about the gifts of the Spirit, my authority in Christ, the power of God's Word and so many other things that I would not have fully appreciated any other way.

However, very few cases are as complex as this one. I have dealt with about four really tough cases in fifteen years out of about 200 that I have personally done. I have ministered deliverance to thousands of people in public meetings all over the world. The Lord is also moving me on all the time in this ministry. I receive words of knowledge so easily now whereas I used to struggle in that area. Ministering deliverance in a personal way to so many people has sharpened my spirit for every aspect of ministry. To God be the glory!

Jesus said:

'In my name shall they cast out devils.' (Mark 16:17)

I can certainly testify to that.

Case 5: A Dog in France!

The following story is absolutely true. In 1995 we went to France for a week's holiday. When we arrived at the home where we were staying we had a very warm reception from the precious family. I had stayed there before a few times on missions. The family had two dogs. One was a tiny poodle and the other was a huge dog. The moment I stepped through the door this big dog began growling at me. He was fine with my wife and children. Over the next couple of days James (the big dog) became worse and worse towards me. I told my family that I was going to have to cast a devil out of him very soon. I chose my time wisely, not knowing what our French family would think of me delivering their dog! James was completely set free almost as soon as I rebuked the demon. He changed instantly towards me and was very affectionate for the rest of the holiday. The owner found out what I had done and said that if I cast anything else out of him he will be useless as a guard dog. We all laughed. Jesus gave us authority to use wherever and whenever we need to.

My pastor tells the story of when he was on his farm many years ago. He found himself alone in a field with a bull charging towards him and with no time to escape. He commanded the bull to stop in the name of Jesus and the bull stopped and bowed down to him!

Use the authority that God has given you to set the captives free and to help mankind in whatever way possible.

Chapter 9

The Doctrine of Deliverance

If we are going to understand deliverance then we must realise that man is made up of three parts – body, soul and spirit. Examine the following Scriptures:

> *'For the word of God is quick, and powerful, and sharper than any two-edged sword, piercing even to the dividing asunder of soul and spirit, and of the joints and marrow, and is a discerner of the thoughts and intents of the heart.'* (Hebrews 4:12)

> *'And the very God of peace sanctify you wholly; and I pray God your whole* **spirit** *and* **soul** *and* **body** *be preserved blameless unto the coming of our Lord Jesus Christ.'* (1 Thessalonians 5:23)

When a person is born again their human spirit is regenerated or made alive unto God (Titus 3:5; Ephesians 2:1–8). Their body and soul were already alive enabling them to exist in the world. Now, once a person is born again their spirit has Christ Jesus dwelling in it which is a no-go area for the devil. However, since their soul and body were alive in the world since they were born they have attracted what you might call 'squatters'. This does not mean demon possession. The word possession implies being completely dominated by the devil. A Christian who is truly born again is not possessed by the devil. He belongs to Jesus. Praise God. However, we all need to be cleaned up in our mind, emotions, body (infirmities) and subconscious. Our thought patterns are far from in line with God when we first get saved! The truth of the Word of God along with freedom in the spirit through deliverance brings us back to thinking properly.

Therefore when someone is being delivered they are simply getting rid of excess baggage that they have either picked up from the world themselves or which has been passed down to them from parents or grandparents. That is all! It is really very simple. Don't try to complicate this subject.

After many years of dealing with this ministry I have noticed that other people take a different line and approach to the way in which we minister. That is fine! The Holy Spirit leads every ministry in unique ways. We never criticise the way other people operate in deliverance. I will say this, however, if you are seeking deliverance. Do not be ministered to by many trains of thought. Stick to just one ministry that you are happy with and **stay with it until you are totally free**. Never give up. Sometimes it seems like a long slow road. But it is worth it in the end.

Jesus said:

> *'If ye continue in my word, then are ye my disciples indeed; And ye shall know the truth, and the truth shall make you free ... If the Son therefore shall make you free, ye shall be free indeed.'*
>
> (John 8:31, 32, 36)

One of the things that you will notice when you are heavily bound is that you can hear the Word and receive it into your mind but you do not get what we call **revelation knowledge** of the Word because of the bondage. This is one of the reasons for binding people up: to stop them from enjoying their inheritance. Those of you who have had some freedom will notice that you can receive and understand the Word much easier and thus grow up spiritually. You can preach to someone who is still bound about who they are in Christ or how to operate in faith and then ask them afterwards what they have gained and it is obvious that they do not have it by revelation. I have seen this over and over again. However, once a person gets free they can receive the Word easily and thus live a victorious life in the earth.

My wife has often said to me that she knew that the real person was locked up inside of her and was stopped from coming out. That is one of the best descriptions I have ever heard of, to describe what a person goes through who needs major deliverance. It is such a joy to see the real person of Ruth Newport emerging and becoming a new creation as God intended. Most people have not even been aware that she needed such a lot of deliverance.

I am convinced that the Holy Spirit Himself has to reveal to someone that they need such ministry. I have heard many people say to me, 'I don't believe that I need deliverance.' Then, shortly afterwards you see the same person being prayed for for deliverance. The penny has dropped. They can now be free.

No wonder Jesus spent about one third of **His** ministry casting out demons!

Principle Demonic Entry Points

Voluntary

Abortion, addictions (drugs, alcohol, smoking, gambling, overeating), alternative medicines (vast majority), behaviour/attitudes, blatant sin, contact with the dead, false religions and cults, immoral sexual acts, objects and buildings, direct occult, pornography, self-curses, ungodly soul-ties, violence.

Involuntary

Ancestral/generational sin, curses, domination, eating disorders, fears and phobias, infirmity/affliction, miscarriages, rejection, sexual abuse, spiritualism/witchcraft, trauma/emotional crises, ungodly soul-ties, violence against self.

False religions check-list

Buddhism, Christian science, Freemasonry, Hare Krishna, Islam, Mormons, Shintoism, Transcendental Meditation, Christadelphianism, Confucianism, Gurus, Hinduism, Jehovah's Witnesses, Moonies, Spiritualism.

Occult check-list

Acupuncture, astral projection, astrology, automatic writing, black magic, black mass, card readings, clairvoyance, colour therapy, divining, ESP, glass ball gazing, Halloween, handwriting analysis, horoscopes, hypnosis, I Ching, iridology, levitation, Martial Arts, numerology, occult literature, ouija boards, pagan objects, pagan rites, palmistry, phrenology, planchettes, predictions, psychic healing, psychic power and awareness, Satanism, Scientology, Shiatsu, Spiritualist healing, Spiritualism, summoning spirits, superstitions, Tarot cards, tea leaf reading, telekinesis, trance dancing, some television programmes (be selective), wearing charms (lucky objects), white magic, witchcraft, yoga.

In the light of the above ways in which the enemy attacks mankind it is hardly surprising just how many people need freedom in one or many areas of the above.

At this point I would like to share a brief incident that happened to me many years ago regarding a dear old lady who lived on her own. She asked if I could go and visit her sometime since she had a problem. I went to see her and we talked. She had been a Christian for a number of years but had never been baptised in the Holy Spirit. I prayed with her but nothing happened. I was determined to get to the bottom of this. She also told me that she had 'things' jumping over her bed at night which kept her awake and caused her to be afraid. I asked to go into her bedroom. When I went into the bedroom her bed was surrounded by crucifixes, holy water and religious objects. I told her to destroy everything and she did. A friend of hers who was a Roman Catholic had been giving her these objects for years. I also took authority over the spirits and told them to leave. I went back to visit her the next week and she had destroyed all the rosary beads, crucifixes, holy water and all the other objects from Rome. All the demons were gone. I then prayed again for her to be filled with the Spirit and she was gloriously baptised in the Holy Spirit and spoke in tongues to the Glory of God. I have since made it clear that all religious objects in Christian homes, should be destroyed.

Ruth and I used to each wear a cross around our necks because we were Christians. I wondered about them in the light of the Scripture:

'Thou shalt not make thee any graven image, or any likeness of any thing that is in heaven above, or that is in the earth beneath, or that is in the waters beneath the earth.' (Deuteronomy 5:8)

We asked the Lord if we should remove them. They were both solid silver. Within a few days of praying they both broke in places that could not be mended. We got rid of them and strongly advise all Christians to do the same.

'We walk by faith, not by sight.' (2 Corinthians 5:7)

PART FOUR

Spiritual Warfare

Chapter 10

Spiritual Warfare

The Bible has a lot to say about war, warfare and military activity. Here are a few verses in the Old Testament:

> *'The LORD is **a man of war**: the LORD is his name.'*
> (Exodus 15:3)

> *'And Moses said unto them, If ye will do this thing, if ye will go armed before the LORD to **war**, and will go all of you armed over Jordan before the LORD, until he hath driven out his enemies from before him.'*
> (Numbers 32:20–21)

> *'And they made **war** ... for they cried to God in the battle ... For there fell down many slain, because the war was of God.'* (1 Chronicles 5:19–22)

Anyone who reads the Old Testament will quickly realise that all the warfare described is on a physical plane and not a spiritual one. However, we can see a type of spiritual warfare in the Old Testament. For instance with the Philistines who were constantly attacking Israel, and anything to do with the Lord.

In the New Testament we see that the battle is no longer on the physical plane but the spiritual:

> *'For we wrestle not against flesh and blood, but against principalities, against powers, against the rulers of the darkness of this world, against spiritual wickedness in high places.'* (Ephesians 6:12)

> *'For though we walk in the flesh, we do not **war** after the flesh: (For the weapons of our warfare are not carnal, but mighty through God to the pulling down of strongholds.)'* (2 Corinthians 10:3–4)

> *'This charge I commit unto thee, son Timothy, according to the prophecies which went before on thee, that thou by them mightest **war** a good **warfare**.'*
> (1 Timothy 1:18)

We are therefore no longer fighting with the arm of the flesh but instead our fight is in the spiritual realm against demonic forces.

Different Levels of Spiritual Warfare

Every Christian is involved in some way or another with spiritual warfare. We all have to resist temptation when it comes our way. We are actually resisting evil spirits whenever we are tempted to sin. Those of us in ministry are often exposed to more attack than others because of the influence that we can have to touch many people for the Gospel. Every time you move up in the body of Christ you will have to deal with a new level of personal spiritual warfare. David gives us a good type of this in the Old Testament:

> *'And when the Philistines heard that David was anointed king over Israel, all the Philistines went up to seek David. And David heard of it, and went out against them.'* (1 Chronicles 14:8)

Read the rest of the chapter for encouragement!

The next type of spiritual warfare that we encounter is in homes and buildings. As a pastor I have been asked by many people to visit their homes to deliver them from evil spirits. This is very real. I will now share from experience some instances of this. I went to one person's home and they described how demons were manifesting in different parts of the house. In this case it turned out that the wife had been heavily involved in the occult for many years and needed much deliverance. She also had Tarot cards and other occult material in her possession. All such material must be burned (Acts 19:19).

The next case involves our present building that we now use as our church, offices and ministry headquarters. We moved into the building which consisted of 22 offices on the second floor of a building in the city centre. It needed some alterations before we could use it for a church. During this time one of our members who was painting the interior noticed a strange smell from time to time at different places. This was very odd. Others then began reporting a disgusting smell in varied places. I decided to pray over the building and take authority over the powers of darkness. Then the Holy Spirit showed me that a particular spirit came out at night and roamed around the corridors. By this time other strange things were happening and so, along with an intercessor, we prayed over the building at night. I could sense evil beings roaming around and asked the Lord for words of knowledge to identify them. We dealt with all that God showed us apart from one. I knew that this was the chief or strong man and asked for his name. The Lord gave me his name as Apollyon which means 'destroyer' (Revelation 9:11). *Strong's Concordance* suggests him to be Satan himself since he is the king of the bottomless pit.

I talked to the Lord about this demon and I felt the Holy Spirit say to me that this spirit is a church destroyer and he was there to destroy our church. It is interesting to note that two churches have closed down in the centre of our city in the past 10 years! I believe that this spirit was responsible for this. I named him and took authority in the name of Jesus Christ. I saw him leave and report to his commanding officer who then sent a 'special agent' to spy on us. God showed this all to me in vision and I bound this spirit also and told him to go. We have never had a single problem with the building since. There is just a wonderful sense of perfect peace in the building for us to worship God in Spirit and truth. Hallelujah!

Another instance was on holiday recently in Wales. We went to our usual farmhouse cottage that we have stayed at many times before. When we arrived the owners told me that they had had nothing but trouble with the cottage. Things kept going wrong. I thought nothing of it because I was on holiday and was not particularly thinking in terms of deliverance. On the Saturday night my wife and I were relaxing in the lounge when I began to sense a demonic presence. I tried to ignore it and we went to bed. It came into our bedroom and I bound it in the name of Jesus Christ and cast it out of the house. We had a peaceful week with no more demons. However, most people just stay from Saturday to Saturday but we were staying until the Monday. On the Sunday night the demon came back expecting us to have gone, no doubt. I rebuked it again and it had such a shock I saw it running away down the lane. I doubt if it will ever be back!

As a born again Christian you have power and authority over these evil beings and it is our job to deal with them whenever they come against us. They will never go until they are told to.

The next type of spiritual warfare is Territorial Warfare. Villages, towns, cities and nations are controlled by different kinds of demons. After many years of developing in deliverance ministry the Lord moved me on to dealing more and more with these Territorial Spirits. I will make a comment at this point and say that this kind of ministry must be exercised by mature believers who are well established and under the covering of their own local church. This is **war**. We have to progress in stages as the Lord leads us. Don't try handling an atomic bomb before learning how to use your hand gun! God is a God of Divine Order and He has a developmental process for all of us. Always talk to your pastor or leadership before embarking on any aspect of Spiritual Warfare at this level.

Why Spiritual Warfare Precedes Revival and Subsequent Reformation

Paul says to the church at Corinth:

> *'But if our gospel be hid, it is hid to them that are lost: in whom **the god of this world hath blinded the minds** of them which believe not, lest the light of the glorious gospel of Christ, who is the image of God, should shine unto them.'*   (2 Corinthians 4:3–4)

This verse shows us clearly that if we can deal with the

root cause of spiritual blindness then people will receive the gospel easily. The light of the gospel speaks so clearly to hearts that are open. The key is to get people to open up in the first place. This is why spiritual warfare is so important.

Paul is saying that if we can deal with the devil who is blocking the mind then evangelism is easy. This is why prayer is so important for unsaved people because without it we are wasting our time. Dr David Yonggi Cho says that there are three things that are necessary to do for revival. Pray. Pray. Pray!

Once you get into prayer the Lord will lead you on by His Spirit into different ways of praying. Always use the Word of God as a basis for all your praying.

Chapter 11

International Spiritual Warfare

As I've already mentioned, many years ago I read a book by a well known preacher and he talked about seeing into the spirit realm. He mentioned seeing angels and demons in vision form which helped him considerably in helping people and in spiritual warfare. As soon as I read that this was possible for us, I prayed and asked the Lord if I could be allowed to 'see' into the spirit realm. About six years later I began seeing demonic activity, and then angels through vision and in reality. My prayers were answered!

In 1993 God began to send me to other nations which was a real surprise to me, since I have never wanted to travel abroad at all. In fact while I was on a train from Geneva to Bern the Lord told me that He wanted me to go to all the capital cities of the world to engage in spiritual warfare. These 'capitals' are not always the recognised capitals as we know them. For instance, New York is not the recognised capital city of America but it is a strategic place for strongholds between USA and the UK and so I was sent there to break international soul-ties between the two nations, among other things!

During my travels abroad I have been privileged to

'see' into the spirit realm on many an occasion. Here are a few instances.

Rome

I was travelling with a friend called Peter through Europe from Bern, Switzerland to Rome on the night sleeper. We arrived at the train station in Rome and started to look for a hotel. A man came up to us and offered us a reasonably priced hotel and we walked with him to the hotel Gabriella. We thought that he may have been an angel since he seemed to vanish. On the way to the hotel I saw a demon spirit watching us. He was afraid of us because he could see our warring angels with us. I watched him go and report back to his leader who told him to keep an eye on us. God had spoken to me on the train and told me to rest completely the first day and not to mention why we were in Rome. I was aware that this demon assigned to us was watching us all day and listening to our every word to find out why we were in Rome. We spent the day eating Italian food and taking photos. I then saw in the evening this spirit report back to his boss and say that we were simply tourists on holiday and did not pose a threat. The boss demon then sent the scout on another mission and we were free to perform our mission without any trouble from the enemy.

We then proceeded to the Vatican and while we were walking around the walls the Lord told me to stop and pray. As I prayed I saw a 'rocket' type missile take off at my feet and go over the walls of the Vatican and explode. I then had a vision of Great Britain with hundreds of black demons leaving. Two weeks later I had another vision of Europe with what looked like an octopus sitting on Rome with all of its tentacles spread out over Europe.

However, the one over Britain had died. I was excited. The Lord had told me to smash the Roman Empire over Britain and I did as I was commanded. This is spiritual warfare.

Berlin

The Lord spoke to me and told me to go to Germany in 1995. Obviously I said 'yes' and began to prepare for the trip. One of my friends in the ministry then told me that he had a friend that he would like to introduce to me. He was a pastor from Germany! This happened only about two weeks after God had told me to go there. A divine appointment. The pastor from Germany invited me to come to speak at his church while I was there. I flew to Berlin and was later joined by an assistant from our church named Adam. The following account of spiritual warfare is one of the most graphic displays of angelic combat that I have ever witnessed.

While I was on the plane from Manchester to Berlin I saw in the spirit that two angels were sitting with me. It has become quite a regular experience now to have special angels with me on such missions. I found a hotel and began to plan my mission. I found out where the highest point was in Berlin. (I will explain more about the High Places shortly.) It was a tower which overlooked the whole city. Every major city usually has at least one of these which is frequently used by tourists to view the city. I would like to make a point at this stage regarding foreign territorial spirits. When I began spiritual warfare to the nations I was unknown to the enemy. I used to take them by surprise. However, I now find that these demonic spirits seem to know me as soon as I land in a country. They often speak to me and ask me what I am doing in their country. I just ignore them and keep my mouth shut.

This was certainly the case in Berlin. They were ready for me! I left the hotel and took a tube train to the tower. It was very hot that day. As I walked up to the tower the Holy Spirit allowed me to hear what the demons were saying. 'He's here,' they kept saying. Then I experienced something amazing. I saw into the spirit realm and watched the demonic system at work. I can only describe it like a major company with different levels of management. I watched as a lesser demon went to tell his upline that I was at the tower. He then went to tell another demon of greater rank. This happened about three times until they reached a high ranking demon. This top spirit gave an order to create a problem at the ticket booth to give them more time to prepare for me. I was approaching the ticket booth when the most awesome thing happened. There were only about seven people in the queue to buy tickets. All you do at these places is give your money over and get a ticket. It usually takes a few seconds. For some unknown reason (in the natural) the queue just stopped! I waited and waited and waited. By this time the queue was very long and people were becoming restless. We must have waited twenty minutes for no apparent reason. I was staggered by all this and realise more and more just how much goes on in the spirit realm that we don't see.

Eventually, I was let through along with some angry Germans. They were furious that they had had to wait. While I was in the lift the Holy Spirit spoke to me and told me not to keep back my sword from blood. I knew what He meant. I was beginning to realise how important this mission was! My two angels were with me and I saw them with a rapier-type sword each. I decided to go to the toilets to engage in warfare. There were so many people around that it would have been awkward anywhere else. I wasn't prepared for what happened next. There was a sign up in German on all the toilets with a lady standing outside preventing anyone from entering. Now I knew why there was a delay at the bottom. It was to allow the powers of darkness time to hinder my mission. I then decided to go up to the restaurant to buy a coffee and pray up there. That was closed as well! There were just crowds of people everywhere and no place for private prayer. I then decided to take some photos and look like a tourist. I walked around the circular top and took many shots of Berlin. I have the photos to prove it. During this time I heard the demons say, 'He hasn't done anything yet.' I walked all the way around the top and came back to the toilet area. The lady who had been on guard had left her position and a small boy had opened the toilets (no doubt in desperation!) I shot into them and locked myself in a cubicle. I saw my angels with me and as soon as I began to bind and rebuke the powers of darkness I saw my two angels spring into action. They were waiting for my word.

> *'Bless the LORD, ye his angels, that excel in strength, that do his commandments, hearkening unto the voice of his word. Bless ye the LORD, all ye his hosts; ye ministers of his, that do his pleasure.'*
>
> (Psalm 103:20–21)

I had already been given all the names of the chief demons that I had to deal with. I write them down usually as God gives them to me, so that I don't miss any of them. One of the names was 'the seat of Satan'. I had never heard that before. The next day at church someone told me that during the war Hitler had brought the seat of

Satan back from one of his trips and placed it in Berlin. I had not mentioned this to anyone. God was confirming to me what had happened the previous day. This often happens.

While I was engaging in warfare, I watched my angels cut the powers of darkness to shreds with their big swords. Then I had a vision of a huge net all over Germany. I watched as this net came off thus freeing the people of Germany to be able to respond to the Gospel. After I finished praying I left the toilets and the lady shouted at me in German. I responded softly in English saying that I didn't understand her. She then told me in broken English that the toilets were closed due to no water in the tower. I hadn't needed any water anyway. My job was finished and I saw my two angels return to me after a few minutes.

I believe that I am called to do what God calls me to do. I do not claim to be the only one doing this kind of work. We all have our place in God's kingdom to do what He says to each of us. Your job is to do what He calls you to do. Don't copy me or anyone else. Find out what your place is in the body of Christ and give yourself fully to it.

Bombay, India

In 1995 I went to Australia via Singapore. I flew with Singapore Airlines and made a scheduled stop at Bombay. As we were coming in to Bombay I was wondering what the demonic strongholds were like since India claims to have literally millions of gods. The Lord knew my thoughts and spoke to me and said that the demons in India were as nothing compared with the demons in Rome! The Lord then gave me three chief spirits to deal with.

We stopped to pick up a few passengers which took about an hour. We were all told to stay on the plane, and I began to pray against the three strongholds. After I had prayed I saw a vision of what looked like missiles shoot into the air and bind the three chief spirits. I then saw all three demons fall down. I had never seen binding before. It was really encouraging to see such graphic visions of the spiritual war that was going on. It is different every time I do it.

When I returned to England after my trip there was a letter waiting for me. It was from a pastor in India. While I was in combat over his country he was in New York and someone gave him a copy of one of my first books *From Victory to Victory*. He enjoyed the book and so invited me to India to preach in his churches. That was ample confirmation of the spiritual warfare over India but then something else happened. One day the telephone rang and a lady from India wanted to come and talk to me about how she could become a real Christian! She was a Hindu from birth and had been seeking the Lord for some time. She had tried other churches but did not find what she was looking for. It is interesting to note that the main spirit that I dealt with over India was Kali the ruling Hindu spirit. This was another confirmation to me. The lady is now in our church and doing very well. Praise the Lord!

Norway

When you book flights to go to different places you often have to stop *en route* for various reasons. This is a golden opportunity to pray over that country and do some warfare if commanded to. I have found that the Lord arranges all of my trips strategically with this in mind.

In January of 1995 I went on a conference with a colleague to Sweden. On the way we stopped at Oslo in Norway. The Lord gave me a series of words of knowledge to pray over Norway. When we were at the airport I saw in the spirit a Viking spirit come against me after I had dealt with some strongholds. I spoke directly to him and a most interesting thing happened. The Viking spirit spoke back to me and said, 'I don't want to go but I know that if you insist then I will have to leave.' He said it in a very irritable and rough way. I told him that I insisted that he leave and I saw him go in the spirit over a hill with another demon with him.

Jamaica

We flew from Manchester to New York and had to change planes for Miami before catching the short flight to the Caribbean Island of Jamaica. The flight to New York was the longest transatlantic flight I had ever known. It took eight and a half hours because we flew in a 757 which is a relatively slow plane. When we arrived at New York we only had about eight minutes before our connecting flight to Miami took off. It looked impossible since we had to get through customs, obtain boarding passes, pass through the metal detector etc. This would normally take at least 20 minutes. Missing this flight would have delayed our arrival in Jamaica. Miraculously we found ourselves on the Miami flight with one minute to spare. I still don't know how we made it. God did some miracles that day! Anyway, I am telling you all this for a reason. God's timing is always perfect. As we were coming into Kingston Airport the Lord spoke to me and told me to rest completely for two days before doing anything. We had never been to Jamaica before and did not know where to go. It was late at night. We told the taxi driver to take us to a hotel near the centre of the city. He took us to an excellent hotel at just the right price.

Peter and I then took two days to recover from the journey. We made a telephone call to the Full Gospel Businessmen's Fellowship and asked when there would be a meeting. They said that their next meeting was at the hotel Pegasus on the Thursday at noon. They asked me to be the speaker to which I agreed. We then found out that the hotel Pegasus was right next door to where we were staying. Not only that but it is also the highest point in Kingston for spiritual warfare. God knows what He is doing. Also, we landed on the Monday night and God had said to rest for two days which took us up to the Thursday. What a mighty God we serve! We were able to engage in spiritual warfare and attend the meeting without striving. At the meeting we were asked to go to other meetings and so doors were opened. I am realising more and more how important it is to obey God when He speaks. We are only servants of **His** instructions.

Chapter 12

Spiritual Warfare in High Places

When we read through the Bible one interesting theme to note is the **high places** in the Old and New Testaments. At the time of Jesus' temptation in the wilderness the devil takes Jesus to two high places!

> *'Then the devil taketh him up into the holy city, and setteth him on a pinnacle of the temple ... Again, the devil taketh him up into an exceeding high mountain, and sheweth him all the kingdoms of the world, and the glory of them.'* (Matthew 4:5, 8)

In Ephesians Paul says,

> *'For we wrestle not against flesh and blood, but against principalities, against powers, against the rulers of the darkness of this world, against* **spiritual wickedness in high places.***'* (Ephesians 6:12)

I believe that the high places have always been a target for the devil to control. The Lord had to destroy the satanic images, idols etc. from the high places time and again. For instance,

> *'And I will destroy your high places, and cut down your images, and cast your carcasses upon the carcasses of your idols, and my soul shall abhor you.'*
>
> > (Leviticus 26:30)

> *'And it came to pass on the morrow, that Balak took Balaam, and brought him up into* **the high places of Baal***, that thence he might see the uttermost part of the people.'* (Numbers 22:41)

When The Lord was giving the commandment to Moses regarding entering the land of Canaan He said,

> *'Then ye shall drive out all the inhabitants of the land from before you, and destroy all their pictures, and destroy all their molten images, and quite* **pluck down all their high places***.'* (Numbers 33:52)

See also Deuteronomy 33:29; 2 Samuel 22:34 and 1 Kings 3:2. You could also look up 'high places' in a *Strong's Concordance* and do a study yourself.

The high places are still used to this day for the purpose of high occult practices such as witchcraft and Satanism. The devil never does anything creative. He usually copies from God and injects evil into it. So it is with the high places. Isaiah says,

> *'For thus saith the* **high and lofty One** *that inhabiteth eternity, whose name is Holy;* **I dwell in the high and holy place***, with him also that is of a contrite and humble spirit, to revive the spirit of the humble, and to revive the heart of the contrite ones.'* (Isaiah 57:15)

The Lord met Moses at the burning bush upon the high place (Exodus 3:1–2). God also met Moses on mount

Sinai to give him the ten commandments (Exodus 19 and 20):

> *'And the LORD came down upon mount Sinai, on the top of the mount: and the LORD called Moses up to the top of the mount; and Moses went up.'*
> (Exodus 19:20)

The Lord also met with Elijah upon mount Horeb (1 Kings 19:7–12). At this point in Elijah's ministry God gave him two very important instructions. He had to anoint Jehu as King and Elisha to take over the prophet's office. This was probably the most important task in his life (1 Kings 19:16).

In the New Testament we often see Jesus going up into the mountains either to pray alone or to take his disciples with Him (Matthew 5:1; 8:1; 14:23; 15:29). Also when Jesus was transfigured before His disciples it was on a mountain:

> *'And after six days Jesus taketh Peter, James, and John his brother, and bringeth them up into **an high mountain** apart, and was transfigured before them.'*
> (Matthew 17:1–2)

Therefore, we can see that the geographical high places have been both a target for evil and also a meeting place for God and His people.

Spiritual Sensitivity

> *'But strong meat belongeth to them that are of full age, even those who by reason of use have their senses exercised to **discern both good and evil**.'*   (Hebrews 5:14)

As we grow in spiritual things we develop spiritual sensitivity to be able to discern what is of God and what is of the devil. One of the things that I notice now after many years of filling my life with God's Word, prayer and fasting, is that when I go into a different territory I can usually discern the spiritual temperature. Some places feel relatively free and other places are in need of much warfare. This is particularly true when I go up to a new high place. I can normally tell what the spiritual climate is like. Sometimes I get attacked by demonic opposition when going up a building or mountain. Obviously, whenever this happens I simply bind the demon and cast it away.

When I visit a different city one of the first things that I do is to locate the high place. This is either going to be a tall building or a mount close by that often overlooks the city. In Paris it was the Eiffel Tower. In Edinburgh it was the castle. In Cape Town, South Africa, it was Table Mountain. In Hobart, the capital city of Tasmania, Australia, I went up the mountain overlooking Hobart.

In September 1995, after visiting almost every capital city in Europe and Britain, I knew that the time had come for me to visit London. I had been to Dublin, Cardiff and Edinburgh at the command of the Lord and I knew that London would be last. Peter and I decided to go on the train and return the same day. On the way down I said to Peter that I would like to go to the top of Westminster Abbey to engage in spiritual warfare over both religious and political affairs as the Houses of Parliament were nearby. Peter said that it was impossible to go up to the top of Westminster Abbey. I replied that I was going to find a way up, but Peter kept insisting that it would not be possible.

We arrived in London on a glorious day during the hottest summer since records began. At Westminster Abbey we had a pleasant surprise. It was true that the general public were not allowed to go to the top inside. However, outside the Abbey, it was being sand-blasted. There was scaffolding all around it and there was a temporary lift to the top which was open to the public for a small fee. God's timing is perfect! If we had not have gone that day we might never have had that kind of an opportunity again. It pays to listen to the Holy Spirit.

We put on the compulsory plastic helmet and were hoisted to the top. It was absolutely perfect. We were right at the top of the Abbey and had a wonderful view of Big Ben and the Houses of Parliament. I had a tremendous time of prayer for our nation and engaged in much spiritual warfare. I would like to mention that it had not rained for about six weeks until that day. Everyone was wearing suitable summer clothing of shorts and T-shirts. Within one hour of us praying the weather changed dramatically. Big black clouds appeared and a storm of torrential rain drenched London. This is quite a normal sign after praying against major strongholds. I have seen extreme changes in the weather on numerous occasions now all over the world. So much so that if there is no change in the weather it is exceptional!

The Ichabod Spirit

The city where our church is located is on top of a hill. I believe that the Lord placed us there for a specific reason to deal with major powers of darkness that have controlled Stoke-on-Trent for many years. One day while I was praying in our church I saw a huge demonic spirit sitting all over the centre of Hanley. I asked the Lord for his name and God said that his name was Ichabod which means *'the glory has departed'* (1 Samuel 4:21–22).

I took authority over it and saw it leave our city. We have been in many prayer meetings where we have had to engage the powers of darkness in direct combat and tell them to loose our city. One day while we were having a crusade in the city, we were praying. All of a sudden everyone was touched by the Holy Spirit and could not move. I then entered the spirit realm. I saw two angels come to me and take me up to the crown of our city. I saw a big gate with another angel by the side of the gate. This angel gave me a big key and said that it was the key to the city. I was awed by this experience. I came back into my body and asked the Lord to confirm to me about keys or else I would not share the experience.

Almost as soon as we all sat up (about 12 of us) one of our intercessors dropped her keys in front of me. Then immediately afterwards another of our fellowship came into the room carrying a bunch of keys with one big key sticking out which looked just like the one in the vision. I had had my confirmations and so shared it with those praying. Everyone was so excited. I believe that evangelism is going to get easier and easier as the devil looses his grip on our city. Hallelujah!

I would like to say that spiritual warfare is only one of the ingredients needed to bring about revival. We also need evangelism, unity, love, follow-up, and other types of prayer.

If God calls you to this type of ministry either locally, nationally or internationally, then take up the challenge with joy and make sure that you have a strong church to back you in prayer and covering. Stay close to the Lord in your own personal life and do as the writer to the Hebrews says:

> '... *waxed valiant in fight, turned to flight the armies of the aliens.*' (Hebrews 11:34)

Further Information

Further information and copies of the Deliverance Questionnaire can be obtained from:

Life-Changing Ministries
Bemersley House
Gitana Street
Hanley
Stoke-on-Trent
ST1 1DY